FTCE® General Knowledge Test Strategy

Winning Multiple Choice Strategies for the FTCE General Knowledge Test

Published by

Complete TEST Preparation Inc.

Copyright © 2015 by Complete Test Preparation Inc. ALL RIGHTS RESERVED.

No part of this book may be reproduced or transferred in any form or by any means, graphic, electronic, or mechanical, including photocopying, recording, web distribution, taping, or by any information storage retrieval system, without the written permission of the author.

Notice: Complete Test Preparation Inc. makes every reasonable effort to obtain from reliable sources accurate, complete, and timely information about the tests covered in this book. Nevertheless, changes can be made in the tests or the administration of the tests at any time and Complete Test Preparation Inc. makes no representation or warranty, either expressed or implied as to the accuracy, timeliness, or completeness of the information contained in this book. Complete Test Preparation Inc. makes no representations or warranties of any kind, express or implied, about the completeness, accuracy, reliability, suitability or availability with respect to the information contained in this document for any purpose. Any reliance you place on such information is therefore strictly at your own risk.

The author(s) shall not be liable for any loss incurred as a consequence of the use and application, directly or indirectly, of any information presented in this work. Sold with the understanding, the author is not engaged in rendering professional services or advice. If advice or expert assistance is required, the services of a competent professional should be sought.

The company, product and service names used in this publication are for identification purposes only. All trademarks and registered trademarks are the property of their respective owners. Complete Test Preparation Inc. is not affiliated with any educational institution.

ISBN-13: 9781772451160

Version 3.1 February 2016

The FTCE General Knowledge exam is administered by the Florida Department of Education, which was not involved in the production of, and do not endorse, this product.

Published by
Complete Test Preparation

Victoria BC Canada
Visit us on the web at http://www.test-preparation.ca
Printed in the USA

About Complete Test Preparation Inc.

The Complete Test Preparation Team has been publishing high quality study materials since 2005. Thousands of students visit our websites every year, and thousands of students, teachers and parents all over the world have purchased our teaching materials, curriculum, study guides and practice tests.

Complete Test Preparation is committed to providing students with the best study materials and practice tests available on the market. Members of our team combine years of teaching experience, with experienced writers and editors, all with advanced degrees.

Feedback

We welcome your feedback. Email us at feedback@test-preparation.ca with your comments and suggestions. We carefully review all suggestions and often incorporate reader suggestions into upcoming versions. As a Print on Demand Publisher, we update our products frequently.

Find us on Facebook

www.facebook.com/CompleteTestPreparation

Contents

6 **Getting Started**
- The FTCE GK Exam — 6
- A Better Score Is Possible — 7
- Who does well on Multiple-Choice exams? — 9

11 **Types of Multiple-Choice**
- Multiple-Choice Quick Tips — 13

17 **Multiple-choice Step-by-Step**

20 **Multiple-choice Strategy Practice**
- Answer Key — 39
- Reading Comprehension Practice — 52
- Answer Key — 66

75 **English Grammar Multiple-Choice**
- Verb Tense — 75
- Common English Usage Mistakes — 92
- Subject Verb Agreement — 98
- English Grammar Practice Questions — 106
- Answer Key — 117

123 **Basic Math Multiple-Choice**
- Math Multiple-choice Strategy — 123
- Practice Questions — 129
- Answer Key — 135
- Fraction Tips, Tricks and Shortcuts — 141
- Decimal Tips, Tricks and Shortcuts — 145
- Percent Tips, Tricks and Shortcuts — 146

149 **Word Problem Multiple-choice Strategy**
- Types of Word problems — 152
- Practice Questions — 161
- Answer Key — 164

168 **How to Write an Essay**
- Common Essay Mistakes I — 177
- Common Essay Mistakes II — 179
- Writing Concisely — 181
- Avoiding Redundancy — 183

191 **How to Prepare for a Test**
Mental Preparation 194

196 **How to Take a Test**
Reading the Instructions 196
How to Take a Test - The Basics 197
In the Test Room – What you MUST do! 202
Common Test-Taking Mistakes 209

214 **Conclusion**

214 **Free Ebook Version**

215 **Study Music Special Offer**

Getting Started with the FTCE General Knowledge

CONGRATULATIONS! By deciding to take the FTCE General Knowledge, you have taken the first step toward a great future! Of course, there is no point in taking this important examination unless you intend to do your very best to earn the highest grade you possibly can. That means getting yourself organized and discovering the best approaches, methods and strategies to master the material. Yes, that will require real effort and dedication on your part but if you are willing to focus your energy and devote the study time necessary, before you know it you will be finished the exam with a great mark!

We know that taking on a new endeavour can be a little scary, and it is easy to feel unsure of where to begin. That's where we come in. This study guide is designed to help you improve your test-taking skills, show you a few tricks and increase both your competency and confidence.

The FTCE General Knowledge Test

The FTCE General Knowledge exam is composed of four sections, a written essay, English language skills, mathematics and reading. The English language skills consists of English grammar and usage, sentence structure, vocabulary, punctuation and spelling. The mathematics sections contains High School math, geometry, probability, data analysis and algebra. The reading section consists of reading comprehension.

While we seek to make our guide as comprehensive as possible, note that like all entrance exams, the FTCE GK test might be adjusted at some future point. New material might be added, or content that is no longer relevant or applicable might be removed. It is always a good idea to give the materials you receive when you register a careful review.

Test Strategy

This is a book about improving your score by using proven test strategies. This is a little different from other books such as a study guide, or a practice test. Even though we do provide lots of information to study and practice test questions, this book is about how to tackle multiple choice questions.

But do not worry - that is not all! While you are learning different strategies for answering multiple choice questions, you can also practice your skill at answering reading comprehension test questions English grammar and usage, and basic math, which are half your score!

A Better Score Is Possible

Worried about that big exam coming up? Do you think you're just not a good test-taker, especially when it comes to standardized tests? The good news is that you're not alone. The bad news is that millions of people are left behind through objective testing, simply because they're not good test-takers - even though they may know the material. They don't know how to handle the format well or understand what's expected of them.
This is especially true of the multiple-choice test. Test-takers are given lots of support for taking essay-style tests. They're helped with skills such as grammar and spelling. However, little is offered for the multiple-choice exam. This is despite the fact that thousands of people find multiple-choice to be the most challenging kind of test. Here are some reasons that so many people have difficulties with multiple-choice:

> **The Broad Range.** Because the questions are so short and quick, a lot of ground is covered in the test. Who's to know what to study with so much material covered?
>
> **Time Limits.** Most standardized tests have time limits, which adds an extra layer of pressure.

Trickery. Many test-designers think that it is too easy to guess a multiple-choice question correctly, so they intentionally make the questions tricky.

Bluffing Not Allowed. With an essay test, you can try to bluff your way through it. Not so with multiple-choice. The answer is either right or wrong.

Difficult to Write. It's not easy for a test-writer to design a good multiple-choice test. Because of this, sometimes, they make them overly difficult.

Shuffled Content. Multiple-choice tests tend to throw the questions in at random, in no particular order. You could be answering a question about the 1700s and then about the 2004 Presidential election.

These challenges mean that students have to be familiar with a wider range of material than on other kinds of exams. You'll need to know specific vocabulary, rules, names, dates, etc.

There are, however, a few advantages to you, the test-taker, with a multiple-choice test. For instance, because there are more multiple-choice items on a test than there are other types, each question tends to have a lower point value. You can afford to miss a few and still be okay. Also, if you're doing a fill-in-the blank or essay test, you have to rely totally on memory for the answer. With a multiple-choice exam, you know that the correct answer is somewhere in the question. You just have to decide which one it is. Often, seeing the right answer will trigger your memory, and you'll recognize it instantly.

Keep in mind, though, the test-writer knows that one advantage of multiple-choice is the fact the answer is on the page. This leads to many test-writers to include what is called a "distracter." This is a possible answer that is designed to look like the correct answer, but which is actually wrong. We'll talk about this again later, but an example would be the question: "Who is known for posting 95 theses on a church wall?" Among the answers might be Martin Luther and Martin Luther King. Because the student vaguely remembers the name "Martin Luther" from the course materials, there's a chance that he'll select the incorrect "Martin Luther King."

Who Does Well On Multiple-Choice Exams?

With so many challenges working against you on the multiple-choice exam, what's the answer? Is there a way to improve your chances and your score? There is! The point of this book is not to discourage you, but to make you aware that there are strategies and tips that you can incorporate to raise your test score. Before we get into the specific strategies, let's take a general look at who does best on these types of tests.

> **Those who know the material.** This should go without saying, but the thing that will most raise your test score will be if you know the material that's going to be covered. While the strategies we'll discuss later will help you even with questions you're unsure of, the surest thing you can do is learn the rules, dates, names, and concepts that you'll be tested on.
>
> **Those who have a calm, cool demeanor when taking a test.** Panicking can cause you to forget the information you think you know. Confidence goes a long way toward a better mark on multiple-choice.
>
> **Those who meditate or pray before the test.** Don't laugh. It's a known fact that people who meditate or pray, depending on their beliefs, enter a test room more confidently, and do better on the exam.
>
> **Those who operate on logic rather than instinct.** Those who take a multiple-choice test based on instinct will be tempted to overlook the stated facts, and let emotion rule.
>
> **Those who have a system.** Most of the book will deal with this, but you should not just guess randomly on questions you don't know. You must have a systematic strategy.

Types of Multiple-Choice Questions

EVEN IF YOU KNOW THAT A TEST WILL BE MULTIPLE-CHOICE, YOU STILL DON'T KNOW ALL THAT YOU NEED TO KNOW. There are various types of multiple-choice questions. Some tests will use just one of these kinds. Others will use several, or even all of them. Let's examine the various types of multiple-choice questions you are likely to encounter.

1. The "Who, What, Where Question." This is the simplest, most basic form of multiple-choice question. It asks for you to recall a single, simple fact about the material. For instance:

Where did the Wright Brothers fly their first airplane?

    a. Richmond, VA
    b. Kitty Hawk, NC
    c. Charlotte, NC
    d. Philadelphia, PA

The correct answer is B. This question simply asks for you to correctly identify a place name.

2. The "Multiple-Answer" Multiple-choice Question. This one varies from the "Who, What, Where" question in that more than one answer could be correct. It often appears like this:

Which of the following was not a declared war by the U.S. Congress?

I. World War I

II. World War II

III. The Korean War

IV. The Vietnam War

    a. I only
    b. I and II only
    c. III only
    d. IV only
    e. III and IV only

The correct answer here is E; neither the Korean nor Vietnam Wars were declared a war by Congress. These questions are tricky because many people are tempted, when they see a right answer, to select it, without thinking that there might be another answer that's also right.

3. The "Best Answer" Multiple-choice Question. On this type, the there might not be one clear objective answer, but rather, you're required to select the one that comes closest to being right, or closest to what you believe is right. For example:

The factor which was the most to blame for the 1986 explosion of the Space Shuttle Challenger was:

    a. It launched too early in the morning.
    b. The cold weather allowed ice to develop.
    c. The astronauts did not have enough sleep.
    d. The astronauts were not adequately trained.

While it's entirely possible that C or D might have played a role, it's now commonly believed that the cause was the ice which had built up on the Shuttle's "O" rings. Some answers are possible, but B is the best answer.

4. The "Fill in the Blank" Multiple-choice Question. This is frequently used on both grammar and reading comprehension tests. The question is presented as a sentence, with one or two key words left out. You must choose the correct one to fill the blank. Example:

The animals at the zoo _____ by the visitors.

   a. Did not feed
   b. Cannot fed
   c. Should not be fed
   d. Never feeding

The answer is C, since "The animals at the zoo should not be fed by the visitors" is the only one which makes good, grammatical sense.

Most the multiple-choice questions you'll encounter will fall into one above category, although it's possible you might also encounter a strange hybrid of two or three types. During your practice for the test, you should practice on each of these four types.

Multiple-Choice Quick Tips

Before looking at specific strategies in detail, lets first look at some general tips that you can use on any test and on multiple-choice questions in any subject. We will explore some of these in more detail later.

- **Finding Hints without Cheating** Pssst. There is a way to get hints about a question, even as you are taking the test—and it is completely legal. The key: Use the test itself to find clues about the answer. Here is how to do this. If you find that a question stumps you, read the answers. If you find one that uses the language that your teacher or textbook used, there is a good chance that this is the right answer. That is because on complex topics, teachers and books tend to always use the same or similar language.

Another point: Look out for test questions which are like previous questions. Often, you will find the same information used in more than one question.

Occasionally you will find the answer to one question contained in another question - be on the lookout for this type of situation and use it to your advantage.

• **Before you try eliminating wrong answers, try to solve the problem.** If you know for sure that you have answered the question correctly, then obviously there is no need to eliminate wrong choices. If you cannot solve it, then see how many choices you can eliminate. Now try solving it again and see if one of the remaining answers comes close to your answer. Your chances of getting the answer right have now improved dramatically. Elimination is one of the most powerful strategies and we will discuss in more detail, as well as practice below.

• **Skip if you do not know.** If you simply do not know the answer and do not know how to get the answer, mark the question in the margin and come back if you have time.

• **Rule out answers that seem so general that they do not offer much information.** If an answer said, for example, "Columbus came to the West in the spring," it is probably not the right answer.

• **Use "all of the above" and "none of the above" to your advantage.** For "all of the above," you need not check to make sure all options are correct. Just check two of them. If two of the answers are correct, then this probably means they are all correct, and you can select "all." (This, of course, is not always the case, especially if there is also an option for "A and B" or "C and D."). Similarly, with "all of the above" questions, you only have to find one wrong answer, and then you have eliminated two choices - one is the wrong answer, and the other is All of the Above.

• **Let "close" answers be your guide.** The clever test-writer often includes an answer that is almost the correct one, to throw you off. The clever test-taker, however, can use this to his advantage. If you see two options that are strangely similar, then chances are good that one of those is the correct choice. That means you can rule out the other answers—and thus improve your chances. For instance, if two choices are George Washington and George Washington Carver, among Abraham Lincoln and Thomas Edison, there is a good chance that one of the two Washingtons is right. More on this strategy below.

Watch Out For Trick Questions

In general, most questions are what they appear to be and over-analyzing is a pitfall to be avoided. However, most multiple-choice tests contain one or two trick questions for a variety of reasons. A trick question is one where the test-writer intentionally makes you think that the answer is easier than it really is. Test-writers include trick questions because so many people think that they have mastered the techniques of taking a test that they need not study the material. In only a very few cases will a test have more than a handful of trick questions. Often instructors will include trick questions, where you really have to know your stuff inside-out to answer it correctly. This separates the "A" students from the "B+" students, and the "A" students from the "A+" students.

The best way to beat the trick question is to read the question carefully and break it down into parts. Then break it down into individual words. For instance, if a question asks,

> "When a plane crashes on the border between the United States and Canada, where are the survivors buried?"

if you had looked at each word individually, you would have realized that the last word, "survivors," means that the test writer is talking about burying people who are still alive.

Before You Change That Answer ...

You are probably familiar with the concept by now: your first instinct is usually right. That is why so many people, when giving advice about tests, tell you that unless you are convinced that your first instinct was wrong, do not take a chance. In those cases, more people change a right answer to the wrong one more often than they change a wrong answer to a right one.

How to Handle This.

Let's take that advice a step further, though. Maybe you do not always have to leave your first answer, especially if you think there might be a reasonable chance that your second choice was right. Before you go changing the answer, though, go on and do a few questions and clear your thoughts of the problem question. After you have done a few more, go back and start over from the beginning. Then see if the original answer is still the one that jumps out at you. If so, leave it. If your second thought now jumps out at you, then go ahead and change it. If both are equal in your mind, then leave it with your first hunch.

Answering Multiple-Choice Step-by-Step

Here is a test question:

Which of the following is a helpful tip for taking a multiple-choice test?

    a. Answering "B" for all questions.

    b. Eliminate all answers that you know cannot be true.

    c. Eliminate all answers that seem like they might be true.

    d. Cheat off your neighbor.

If you answered B, you are correct. Even if you are not positive about the answer, try to get rid of as many options as possible. Think of it this way: If every item on your test has four possible answers, and if you guess on one of those four answers, you have a one-in-four chance (25%) of getting it right. This means you should get one question right for every four that you guess.

However, if you can get rid of two answers, then your chances improve to one-in-two chances, or 50%. That means you will get a correct answer for every two that you guess.

So much for an obvious tip for improving your multiple-choice score. There are many other tips that you may or may not have considered, which will give your grade a boost. Remember, though, that none of these tips are infallible. In fact, some test-writers who know these suggestions deliberately write questions that can confound your system. Usually, however, you will do better on the test if you put these tips into practice.

By familiarizing yourself with these tips, you increase your chances and who knows; you might just get a lucky break and increase your score by a few points!

Answering Step-by-Step.

It might seem complicated and unnecessary to follow a formula for answering a multiple-choice question. After you have practiced this formula for a while, though, it will come naturally and will not take any time at all. Try to follow these steps below on each question.

Step 1. Cover up the answers while you read the question. See the material in your mind's eye and try to envision what the correct answer is before you expose the answers on the answer sheet.

Step 2. Uncover the responses.

Step 3. Eliminate or Estimate. Cross out every choice that you know is ridiculous, absurd or clearly wrong. Then work with the answers that remain.

Step 4. Watch for distracters. A distracter is an answer that looks very similar to the correct answer, but is put there to trip you up. If you see two answers that are strikingly similar, the chances are good that one of them is correct. For instance, if you are asked the term for the distance around a square, and two of the responses are "periwinkle" and "perimeter," you can guess that one of these is probably correct, since the words look similar (both start with "peri-"). Guess one of these two and your chances of correcting selecting "perimeter" are 50/50. More on this below.

Step 5. Check! If you see the answer that you saw in your mind, put a light check-mark by it and then see if any of the other choices are better. If not, mark that response as your answer.

Step 6. If all else fails, guess. If you cannot envision the correct response in your head, or figure it out by reading the passage, and if you are left totally clueless as to what the answer should be, guess.

Watch out for this strategy if the test you are taking penalizes for wrong answers. Only a few tests do this, and if so, then guessing is NOT a recommended strategy!

There is a common myth that says choice "C" has a statistically greater chance of being correct. This may be true if your professor is making the test, however, most standardized tests today are generated by computer and the choices are randomized. We do not recommend choosing "C" as a strategy.

That is a quick introduction to multiple-choice to get us warmed up. Next we move onto the strategies and practice test questions section. Each multiple-choice strategy is explained, followed by practice questions using the strategy. Opposite this page is a bubble sheet for answering.

Multiple-choice Strategy Practice Questions Answer Sheet.

1. A B C D
2. A B C D
3. A B C D
4. A B C D
5. A B C D
6. A B C D
7. A B C D
8. A B C D
9. A B C D
10. A B C D
11. A B C D
12. A B C D
13. A B C D
14. A B C D
15. A B C D
16. A B C D
17. A B C D
18. A B C D
19. A B C D
20. A B C D
21. A B C D
22. A B C D
23. A B C D
24. A B C D
25. A B C D
26. A B C D
27. A B C D
28. A B C D
29. A B C D
30. A B C D
31. A B C D
32. A B C D
33. A B C D
34. A B C D
35. A B C D
36. A B C D
37. A B C D
38. A B C D
39. A B C D
40. A B C D
41. A B C D
42. A B C D
43. A B C D
44. A B C D
45. A B C D

Multiple-Choice Strategy Practice Questions

THE FOLLOWING ARE DETAILED STRATEGIES FOR ANSWERING MULTIPLE-CHOICE QUESTIONS WITH PRACTICE QUESTIONS FOR EACH STRATEGY.

Answers appear following this section with a detailed explanation and discussion on each strategy and question, plus tips and analysis.

Strategy 1 - Locate Keywords

For every question, figure out exactly what the question is asking by locating key words that are in the question. Underline the keywords to clarify your thoughts and keep on track.

Directions: Read the passage below, and answer the questions using this strategy.

Free-range is a method of farming where animals are allowed to roam freely, instead of being enclosed in a pen. The term is used in two senses that do not overlap completely: as a farmer-centric description of farming methods, and as a consumer-centric description. Farmers practice free-range to achieve free-range or humane certification (and thus capture high prices), to reduce feed costs, to improve the happiness and liveliness of their animals, to produce a higher-quality product, and as a method of raising multiple crops on the same land. [1]

1. The free-range method of farming

a. Uses a minimum amount of fencing to give animals more room.
b. Can refer to two different things.
c. Is always a very humane method.
d. Only allows for one crop at a time.

2. Free-range farming is practiced

a. To obtain free-range certification.
b. To lower the cost of feeding animals.
c. To produce higher quality product.
d. All of the above.

3. Free-range farming:

a. Can mean either farmer described or consumer described methods.
b. Is becoming much more popular in many areas.
c. Has many limits and causes prices to go down.
d. Is only done to make the animals happier and healthier.

4. Free-range certification is most important to farmers because:

a. Free-range livestock are less expensive to feed.
b. The price of the product is higher.
c. Both a and b
d. The animals are kept in smaller enclosures, so more can be produced.

Strategy 2 - Watch Negatives

For every question, no matter what type, look for negatives. These can include never, not, and others that will completely change what is being asked.

Directions: Read the passage below, and answer the questions using this strategy.

Male grizzly bears can weight more than 1,000 pounds, but typically weigh 400 pounds to 770 pounds. Females are on average 38% smaller, about 250–350 pounds, an example of sexual dimorphism. On average, grizzly bears stand about 1 meter (3.3 ft.) at the shoulder when on all fours, and 2 meters (6.6 ft.) on their hind legs, but males often stand 2.44 meters (8 ft.) or more on their hind legs. On average, grizzly bears from the Yukon River area are about 20% smaller than typical grizzlies. [2]

5. Sexual dimorphism does not mean

    a. Male grizzly bears are the same size as the female of the species.

    b. All grizzly bears look the same and are the same size.

    c. Grizzly bears can be quite large, and weigh more than half a ton.

    d. All of the above

6. The size of a full-grown grizzly bear is never

    a. More than 500 pounds.

    b. Depends on the bear's sex.

    c. Determined simply by diet.

    d. More than 6 feet tall.

7. Grizzly bears from the area of the Yukon River do not

   a. Get as big as most other grizzly bears do
   b. Get the rich and varied food supply needed
   c. Need the same nutrients as other grizzly bears
   d. Get less than 7 feet tall, and weigh close to half of a ton

Strategy 3 - Read the Stem Completely

For every question, no matter what type, read the information in the stem and then try to determine the correct answer before you look at the different answers.

Directions: Read the passage below, and answer the questions using this strategy.

Formerly, taxonomists listed brown and grizzly bears as separate species. Technically, brown and grizzly bears are classified as the same species, Ursus Arctos. The term "brown bear" is commonly used to refer to the members of this species found in coastal areas where salmon is the primary food source. Brown bears found inland and in northern habitats are often called "grizzlies." Brown bears on Kodiak Island are classified as a distinct subspecies from those on the mainland because they are genetically and physically isolated. The shape of their skulls also differs slightly. [3]

8. Grizzly bears, brown bears, and kodiak bears are all

   a. Arctas Ursinas
   b. Ursus Arctos
   c. Arctos Ursina
   d. Ursula Arctic

9. Kodiak brown bears are classified as a different subspecies because

a. They are much larger than other brown bears

b. Their diet is radically different from that of other brown bears

c. They are not true brown bears but instead a mixture of bear species

d. Of their genetics and head shape, as well as their physical isolation

10. The term grizzlies, when referring to the brown bear, is used mainly

a. In eastern areas where the bear grows large

b. Only in snowy areas where there are low year round temperatures

c. In the northern and inland areas

d. In areas where the bear has a silver appearance

11. The term brown bear is normally used

a. When one of the main food sources is salmon

b. When the bear is small

c. When the bear is found inland

d. When the bear has a light brown coat and is very large

Strategy 4 - Consider all the Choices Before Deciding

For every question, no matter what type, make sure to read every option before making your choice.

Directions: Read the passage below, and answer the questions using this strategy.

Jim Martell, a hunter from Idaho, reportedly found and shot a grizzly-polar bear hybrid near Sachs Harbor on Banks Island, Northwest Territories, Canada, on April 16, 2006. Martell had been hunting for polar bears with an official license and a guide, at a cost of $50,000, and killed the animal believing it to be a normal polar bear. Officials took interest in the creature after noticing that it had thick, creamy white fur, typical of polar bears, as well as long claws; a humped back; a shallow face; and brown patches around its eyes, nose, and back, as well as patches on one foot, which are all traits of grizzly bears. If the bear had been adjudicated to be a grizzly, he would have faced a possible CAN$1,000 fine and up to a year in jail. A DNA test conducted by the Wildlife Genetics International in British Columbia confirmed that it was a hybrid, with the mother a polar bear and the father a grizzly. It is the first documented case in the wild, though it was known that this hybrid was biologically possible and other hybrids have been bred in zoos in the past. [4]

12. Which grizzly bear features did the hybrid bear have?

    a. Brown patches in certain areas

    b. Long claws

    c. A shallow face

    d. All of the above

13. The hybrid bear was the result of

    a. A male brown bear and a female grizzly.

    b. A female brown bear and a male grizzly bear.

    c. A female polar bear and a male grizzly bear.

    d. A male polar bear and a female grizzly.

14. The hybrid bear tested in this case was

    a. The first case ever known where two different bear species mated successfully.

    b. Genetically flawed and prone to many diseases and conditions.

    c. A fluke, and a mistake of nature which has never happened.

    d. The first proof of a wild bear hybrid species outside of zoos.

15. Modern science

    a. Has proven that the cubs from two different species will not survive in almost every case.

    b. Has known for some time that these hybrid bears were possible.

    c. Completely understands how bear hybrids occur and why this happens in nature.

    d. Has studied hundreds of bear hybrids in an attempt to learn more.

Strategy 5 - Elimination

For every question, no matter what type, eliminating obviously incorrect answers narrows the possible choices. Elimination is probably the most powerful strategy for answering multiple-choice.

Directions: Read the passage below, and answer the questions using this strategy.

The male peafowl, or peacock, has long been known and valued for its brilliant tail feathers. The bright spots on it are known as "eyes," and inspired the Greek myth that Hera placed the hundred eyes of the slain giant Argus on the tail of her favorite bird. Indian Peafowl are iridescent blue-green or blue in the head, neck and breast.

The back, or scapular, feathers are vermiculated in black and white, while the primaries are orange-chestnut. The so-called "tail" of the peacock, also termed the "train," is not the tail quill feathers but highly elongated upper tail feathers. It is mostly bronze-green, with a series of eyes that are best seen when the train is fanned. The actual tail feathers are short and grey-colored and can be seen from behind when a peacock's train is fanned in a courtship display.

During the molting season, the males shed their stunning train feathers and reveal the unassuming grey-colored tail, which is normally hidden from view beneath the train. The female peacock is duller in comparison. It is mostly brown, with pale under-parts and some green iridescence in the neck, and lacks the long upper tail feathers of the male. [5]

16. The long colorful tail feathers of the peacock

   a. Are only present in the male of the species
   b. Are used by both sexes to warn off predators
   c. Are normally red and blue in color
   d. Are only present for a very short time each year

17. The differences between the male and female peacock are

   a. Size and weight
   b. Coloring and tail feather length
   c. The female does not ever leave the nest
   d. The male sits on and hatches the eggs

18. The term peacock actually refers to

   a. Both sexes from the pheasant family
   b. The eyes on the tail feathers of the bird
   c. The male bird of the peafowl species
   d. The female bird of the peafowl species

19. The gray tail feathers on the male peacock can be seen

   a. When the bird is startled
   b. Only when the bird is searching for food
   c. When the peacock lowers the tail feathers to the ground
   d. During molting

Strategy 6 - Opposites

For every question, no matter what type, look at answers that are opposites. When two answers are opposites, the odds increase that one of them is the correct answer.

Directions: Read the passage below, and answer the questions using this strategy.

Smallpox is an infectious disease unique to humans, caused by either of two virus variants, the Variola Major or Variola Minor. The disease is also known by the Latin names Variola or Variola vera, which is a derivative of the Latin varius, meaning spotted.

Smallpox localizes in small blood vessels of the skin and in the mouth and throat. In the skin, this results in a characteristic rash, and later, blisters. Variola Major produces a more serious disease and has an overall mortality rate of 30–35%. Variola Minor causes a milder form of disease (also known as alastrim, cottonpox, milkpox, whitepox, and Cuban itch) which kills about 1% of its victims. Long-term complications of Variola major infection include characteristic scars, commonly on the face, which occur in 65–85% of survivors. Blindness and limb deformities due to arthritis and osteomyelitis are less common complications, seen in about 2–5% of cases. [6]

20. Smallpox

    a. Effects all mammals, including humans

    b. Is caused by a bacteria from contact with dead flesh

    c. Was called the great pox during the fifteenth century

    d. Only affects humans, although other species can carry and transmit the virus

21. Smallpox caused by Variola major has a

    a. Thirty to thirty five percent survival rate

    b. Sixty percent mortality rate

    c. Thirty to thirty five percent mortality rate

    d. Sixty percent survival rate

22. Smallpox caused by Variola minor is

   a. Much more severe, with a greater number of pox and more scarring
   b. Much less severe, with fewer pox and less scarring
   c. Characterized because there are no pox
   d. So minor that no treatment or medical attention is needed

23. Smallpox can be fatal

   a. In between thirty and thirty five percent of those who catch the virus, depending on the type
   b. In between thirty and sixty five percent of those who catch the virus, depending on the type
   c. When no medical treatment is available
   d. Only in developing countries where medical care is poor

Strategy 7 - Look for Differences

For every question, no matter what type, look at the two choices that seem to be correct and then examine the differences between the two. Refer to the stem to determine the best answer.

Directions: Read the passage below, and answer the questions using this strategy.

Lightning is an atmospheric discharge of electricity accompanied by thunder, which typically occurs during thunderstorms, and sometimes during volcanic eruptions or dust storms. Atmospheric electrical discharges, or bolts of lightning, can travel at speeds of 130,000 mph, and reach temperatures approaching 54,000° F. This is hot enough to fuse silica sand into glass channels, known as fulgurites, that are normally hollow and can extend some distance into the ground. There are some 16 million lightning storms in the world every year.

The irrational fear of lightning and thunder is astraphobia.

Lightning can also occur within the ash clouds of volcanic eruptions, or can be caused by violent forest fires which generate sufficient dust to create a static charge.

How lightning initially forms is still a matter of debate: Scientists have studied root causes ranging from atmospheric perturbations (wind, humidity, friction, and atmospheric pressure) to the impact of solar wind and accumulation of charged solar particles. Ice inside a cloud is thought to be a key element in lightning development, and may cause a forcible separation of positive and negative charges within the cloud, thus helping in the formation of lightning. [7]

24. Astraphobia is

    a. Fear of thunder

    b. Fear of thunder and lightning

    c. Fear of lightning

    d. None of the above

25. Lightning occurs

    a. Only in thunderstorms

    b. In thunderstorms and dust storms

    c. In thunderstorms, volcanic eruptions and dust storms

    d. In the upper atmosphere

26. Fulgurites are

    a. Made of silica

    b. Made of glass

    c. Made of silica turned in to glass

    d. Made of silica and glass

Strategy 8 - Context clues

Looked at the sentences and the context to determine the best option. Sometimes, the answer may be located right in the passage or question.

Directions: Read the passage below, and answer the questions using this strategy.

Venus is one of the four solar terrestrial planets, meaning that, like the Earth, it is a rocky body. In size and mass, it is very similar to the Earth, and is often described as its "sister," or Earth's twin. The diameter of Venus is only 650 km. less than the Earth's, and its mass is 81.5% of the Earth's. However, conditions on the Venusian surface differ radically from those on Earth, due to its dense carbon dioxide atmosphere. The mass of the atmosphere of Venus is 96.5% carbon dioxide, with most of the remaining 3.5% nitrogen.

Venus is the second-closest planet to the Sun, orbiting every 224.7 Earth days. The planet is named after Venus, the Roman goddess of love and beauty. After the Moon, it is the brightest natural object in the night sky, reaching an apparent magnitude of −4.6. Because Venus is an inferior planet from Earth, it never appears to venture far from the Sun: its elongation reaches a maximum of 47.8°. Venus reaches its maximum brightness shortly before sunrise or shortly after sunset, and is often called the Morning Star or the Evening Star. [8]

27. Apparent magnitude is

    a. A measure of darkness

    b. A measure of brightness

    c. The distance from the moon

    d. The distance from the earth

28. The elongation of a planet is

a. The angular distance from the sun, as seen from earth.
b. The distance from the sun
c. The distance form the earth
d. None of the above

29. Terrestrial planets are

a. Made of rock
b. Have people on them
c. The earth and no others
d. The same size as Earth

30. How many planets orbit the sun in less than 224.7 days?

a. 1 planet
b. Only Venus
c. 2 planets
d. 3 planets

Strategy 9 - Try Every Option

For definition questions, try out all the options - one option will fit better than the rest. As you go through the options, use Strategy 5 - Elimination, to eliminate obviously incorrect choices as you go.

Directions: Read the passage below, and answer the questions using this strategy.

On Earth, common weather phenomena include wind, cloud, rain, snow, fog and dust storms. Less common events include natural disasters such as tornadoes, hurricanes, typhoons and ice storms. Almost all weather phenomena occurs in the troposphere (the lower part of the atmosphere). Weather does occur in the stratosphere and can affect weather lower down in the troposphere, but the exact mechanisms are poorly understood.

Weather occurs primarily due to different temperature and moisture densities. The strong temperature contrast between polar and tropical air gives rise to the jet stream. Weather systems in the mid-latitudes, such as extra-tropical cyclones, are caused by instabilities of the jet stream flow. Weather systems in the tropics, such as monsoons or thunderstorms, are caused by different processes.

Because the Earth's axis is tilted relative to its orbital plane, sunlight is incident at different angles at different times of the year. In June the Northern Hemisphere is tilted towards the sun, so at any given Northern Hemisphere latitude, sunlight is more direct than in December. This effect causes seasons. Over thousands to hundreds of thousands of years, changes in Earth's orbital parameters affect the amount and distribution of solar energy received by the Earth and influence long-term climate. [2]

31. The troposphere is

    a. The highest strata of the atmosphere

    b. The lowest strata of the atmosphere

    c. The middle level of the atmosphere

    d. Not part of the atmosphere

32. Monsoons are

    a. Caused by instabilities in the jet stream

    b. Caused by processes other than instabilities in the jet stream

    c. Part of the jet stream

    d. Cause the jet stream

33. Extra-tropical cyclones occur

    a. In the tropics

    b. In temperate zones

    c. In the gulf stream

    d. In mid-latitudes

34. Tilted means:

    a. Slanted

    b. Rotating

    c. Connected to

    d. Bent

Strategy 10 - Work for it

For questions about supporting details, work is the key. Review the passage to locate the right option. Never forget the choices that you are given are designed to confuse, and they may *seem* reasonable answers. However, if they are not mentioned in the text, they are "red herring" answers.

The best answer is the exact answer mentioned in the text.

Directions: Read the passage below, and answer the questions using this strategy.

Ebola is the common term for a group of viruses belonging to genus Ebola virus (EBOV), which is a part of the family Filoviridae, and for the disease that they cause, Ebola hemorrhagic fever. The virus is named after the Ebola River, where the first recognized outbreak of Ebola hemorrhagic fever occurred.

The viruses are characterized by long filaments, and have a shape similar to that of the Marburg virus, also in the family Filoviridae, and possessing similar disease symptoms. There are several species within the Ebola virus genus, which in turn have several specific strains or serotypes.

The Zaire virus is the type species, which is also the first discovered and the most lethal. Ebola is transmitted primarily through bodily fluids, and to a limited extent through skin. The virus interferes with the endothelial cells lining the interior surface of blood vessels and platelet cells. As the blood vessel walls become damaged and the platelets are unable to coagulate, patients succumb to hypovolemic shock.

Ebola first emerged in 1976 in Zaire. It remained largely obscure until 1989 with the outbreak in Reston, Virginia.[10]

35. The Ebola virus received this name because of

    a. The doctor who first discovered the virus

    b. The cure that is used to treat those infected

    c. The river where the disease was first encountered

    d. What the virus does to the body

36. Viruses in the Ebola genus are recognizable

    a. Because of their hooked shape

    b. Because of their long filaments

    c. Due to their oblong heads

    d. Because of their unique color

37. One of the most common causes of death from the Ebola family of viruses is

    a. Hypovolemic shock due to blood vessel damage

    b. Bleeding of the brain that cannot be stopped

    c. A heart attack from blood loss and lack of fluids

    d. A high fever that cannot be lowered

38. The most deadly strain of the Ebola virus family is the

    a. The Reston strain

    b. The Ivory Coast strain

    c. The Zaire strain

    d. The Sudan strain

Strategy 11 - Look at the Big Picture

Details can be tricky when dealing with main idea and summary questions, but do not let the details distract you. Look at the big picture instead of the smaller parts to determine the right answer.

Directions: Read the passage below, and answer the questions using this strategy.

As of late 2005, three fruit bat species have been identified as carrying the Ebola virus but not showing disease symptoms. They are now believed to be a natural host species, or reservoir, of the virus. Plants, arthropods, and birds have also been considered as reservoirs; however, bats are considered the most likely candidate.

Bats were known to reside in the cotton factory where the first outbreaks in 1976 and 1979 occurred, and they have also been implicated in Marburg infections in 1975 and 1980. Of 24 plant species and 19 vertebrate species experimentally inoculated with Ebola virus, only bats became infected. The absence of clinical signs in these bats is characteristic of a reservoir species.

In 2002-03, a survey of 1,030 animals from Gabon and the Republic of the Congo including 679 bats found Ebola virus RNA in 13 fruit bats (Hypsignathus monstrosus, Epomops franquetti and Myonycteris torquata). Bats are also known to be the reservoirs for several related viruses including Nipah virus, Hendra virus and Lyssa viruses.[11]

39. The species most suspected as a potential Ebola virus reservoir is

    a. Birds
    b. Insects
    c. Plants
    d. Bats

40. Most plant and animal species

   a. Can carry the Ebola virus but not become infected
   b. Can not carry and transmit the Ebola virus
   c. Are responsible for new cases of Ebola viruses
   d. Can be infected with one of the Ebola viruses

41. Bats are known for

   a. Being carriers of many different viruses, including Ebola
   b. Transmitting the Ebola virus through a scratch
   c. Being susceptible to the virus and becoming infected
   d. Transmitting the Ebola virus through infected droppings

Strategy 12 - Best Possible Answer

Try to determine the best possible answer according to the information given in the passage. Do not be distracted by answers that seem correct or are mostly correct.

Directions: Read the passage below, and answer the questions using this strategy.

In the early stages, Ebola may not be highly contagious. Contact with someone in early stages may not even transmit the disease. As the illness progresses, bodily fluids represent an extreme biohazard.

Due to lack of proper equipment and hygienic practices, large-scale epidemics occur mostly in poor, isolated areas without modern hospitals or well-educated medical staff. Many areas where the infectious reservoir exists have just these characteristics.

In such environments, all that can be done is immediately cease all needle sharing or use without adequate sterilization procedures, to isolate patients, and to observe strict barrier nursing procedures with the use of a medical-rated disposable face mask, gloves, goggles, and a gown always. This should be strictly enforced for all medical personnel and visitors. [12]

42. Ebola is highly contagious

   a. Only when blood is present

   b. Only in the first stages before hemorrhaging occurs

   c. At all stages of the illness from incubation to recovery

   d. Only in the later stages when the virus is very numerous

43. Exposure to the Ebola virus means

   a. A death sentence for most patients

   b. Isolation for the patient, and proper precautions for all medical personnel to contain the virus

   c. The virus will spread rapidly and there is no treatment available

   d. A full recovery usually, with very few symptoms

44. Ebola outbreaks commonly occur

   a. Because sterilization and containment procedures are not followed or available

   b. Due to infected animals in the area

   c. Because of rat droppings in homes

   d. Because of a contaminated water supply

45. Ebola is

   a. More common in advanced nations where treatment makes the disease minor

   b. More common in third world and developing countries

   c. Fatal in more than ninety-five percent of the cases

   d. Highly contagious during the incubation period

Answers to Sample Multiple-Choice Strategy Questions

Strategy 1 - Keywords in the question tells what the question is asking

1. B
The question asks about the free range *method* of farming. Here method refers to *type* of farming. "Method" here is the keyword and can be marked or underlined.

2. D
The Question is, "Free-range farming is *practiced* ..." The keyword here is "practiced." Looking at the choices, which all start with "to," it is clear the answer will be about *why* free range ... Also notice that one choice is "All of the above," which here, is the correct answer. However, when "All of the above" is an option, this is a potential Elimination strategy. All you have to do is find one option that is incorrect and you can use Strategy 5 - Elimination to eliminate two choices and increase your odds from one in four, to one in two.

3. A
The question is, "Free range farming husbandry ..." From the question, and the *lack* of keywords, together with the choices presented, the answer will be a definition free range farming husbandry.

4. C
The question is, "Free-range certification is *most important* to farmers because ... " The keywords here are "most important." Be careful to choose the best possible answer.

Strategy 2 - Negatives.

These four questions all have negatives: does not mean, is never, do not, and is not. These questions exclude possibilities, so if you see any choices that are true, you can eliminate them right away.

5. D

The question asks what sexual dimorphism does *not* mean. Circle the word "not" and keep it firmly in mind. Next, what is sexual dimorphism. Reading the text quickly, sexual dimorphism is not defined explicitly, but related to the female bears being smaller than the males. Probably there are other aspects, but this general definition is all that is needed to answer the question.

First, notice that "All of the above" is choice D. In addition the question is a negative. So in order for choice D to be correct, choices A, B and C must be *in*correct. This narrows down your options. If any of choices A, B or C are correct, then you can eliminate that choice as well as choice D.

Either all the choices are *in*correct, in which case, choice D, "All of the above" is correct.

Choice A, male and females are the same size is incorrect. Choice B, all grizzly bears look the same and are the same size, is incorrect. Choice C, grizzly bears (plural so *all* grizzly bears) can be large and weigh more than half a ton. This is incorrect since while all grizzly bears are large, female bears weight less than half a ton.

All three choices are incorrect so choice D is the correct answer, "All of the Above," are incorrect.

6. A

First, circle or underline never to show this is a negative question. Now look at the options to find an option that is not true.

Choice A is true as male bears are 1,000 pounds. Place a mark beside this one. It may be tempting to select this option as your answer, but it is important to look at all choices before making a final decision.

Choice B is not true - size does not depend on the sex.
Choice C is not true - size does not depend on diet.
Choice D is not true - males often stand 8 feet.

So choice A is correct.

7. A
First circle "do not" to mark this as a negative question.

Choice A is correct, Yukon River grizzly bears do not get as big as other grizzlies, so put a mark beside it for later consideration. Examine the other choices before making a final decision.

Choice B is not mentioned in the text, and can be eliminated.

Choice C is not mentioned in the text and can be eliminated.

Choice D is true, but this is a negative question so it is false.

Some of the above choices may be true from a common sense point of view, but if they aren't mentioned specifically in the passage, they can be eliminated.

Choice A is correct.

Strategy 3 - Read the stem completely.

Read the question, and then look for the answer in the text before reading the choices. Reading the choices first will confuse, just as it is meant to do! Do not fall into this trap!

8. B
The choices here are very confusing and are meant to be! Four variations on the latin species name, Ursus Arctos are given, so the question is what version of this latin name is correct, which gives a very straight-forward strategy to solving. Since the name is latin, it is going to stand out in the text. Take the first option, "Arctas Ursinas," and scan the text for something that looks like that. At the end of the second sentence is "Ursus Arctos," which is very close. Next confirm what this sentence refers to, which gives the correct answer, Choice B.

9. D
This question asks why Kodiak brown bears are a different subspecies, and the options are designed to confuse a careless, stressed test-taker. Scan the text for "Kodiak," which appears in the second to last sentence, and answers the question.

10. C
This question asks about the relationship between brown bears and grizzly bears. If you are not careful you will be confused by the choices.

11. A
Read the question, then read the text before trying to answer and avoid confusion.

Strategy 4 - Consider all choices before deciding.

In Strategy 3, we learned to find the correct answer in the text before reading the choices. OK, now you have read the text and have the right answer. The next thing is Strategy 4 - Read *all* of the choices. Once you have read all of the choices, select the correct choice.

12. D
First, notice that "All of the above" is a choice. So if you find one option that is incorrect, you can eliminate that option and option D, "All of the above." Reading the question first, (Strategy #3) then looking in the text, and then reading all of the choices before answering, you can see that choices A, B and C are all correct, so choice D, All of the Above, is the correct choice.
If you had not read all the choices first, then you might be tempted to impulsively choose A, B, or C.

13. C
Looking at the choices, they are designed to confuse with different choices and combinations. Recognizing this, it is therefore important to be extra careful in making your choice. If you are stressed, in a hurry, or not paying attention, you will probably get this question wrong by making an impulsive choice and not reading through all the choices before making a selection.

Referring to the text, you will find the sentence, "... it was a hybrid, with the mother a polar bear and the father a grizzly," which answers the question.

14. D
Reading through all the choices, B and C can be eliminated

right away as they are not referred to in the text. They might appear as good answers but they are not from the passage.

Looking at choices A and D, the issue is if this has happened before, or has it happened only in zoos. Referring to the text, the last sentence tells us the answer, "It is the first documented case in the wild, though it was known that this hybrid was biologically possible and other hybrids have been bred in zoos in the past."

15. B
Reading through the four choices, the question concerns, what does science know? Does it happen all the time? Completely understood? They do survive? Is it possible? Look in the text for how much is known. The last sentence, "It is the first documented case in the wild, though it was known that this hybrid was biologically possible" gives the answer.

Strategy 5 - Elimination.

For every question, no matter what type, eliminating obviously incorrect answers narrows the possible choices. Elimination is probably the most powerful strategy for answering multiple-choice.

16. A
Using this strategy the choices can be narrowed down to choices A and D. I have never seen a peacock with red in their tail, so choice C can *probably* be eliminated, but check back. Most birds and many animals have a pattern where the male is colorful and the female less colorful. Choice B can be eliminated as it refers to "both sexes" having colorful tails. Choice D is a good candidate as the text refers to molting season, however, the text does not say how long this is, so there is some doubt. This makes choice A the best choice as it is referred to directly in the text.

17. B
Choice D can be eliminated right away, as it is rare for a male bird to sit on eggs.

Skimming the passage, choices A and C can be eliminated, as they are not mentioned directly in the text, leaving only choice D.

18. C
Choices A and D can be eliminated right away, since "cock" always refers to a male bird. Referring to the text, "The male peafowl, or peacock, has long been ..." making choice C the best choice.

19. D
Choices A and B can be eliminated either right away or with a quick check of the passage, since they are not mentioned. Choice C is suspicious since the grey feathers are under the tail feathers, so it is difficult to see how they could be visible when the tail feathers are lowered.

Strategy 6 - Opposites

If there are opposites, one of them is generally the correct answer. If it helps, make a table that lays out the different options and the correct option will become clear.

20. D
Notice that choices A and D are opposites. Referring to the text, "Smallpox is an infectious disease unique to humans ..." eliminates choice A. Also notice choices B and C are not mentioned in the text and can be eliminated right away.

21. C
Notice that all the choices are opposites. 30 - 35% mortality, or survival rate, or 60%. Therefore, the task is to review the text, looking for 30% or 60%, survival or mortality, stay clear, and do not get confused. Sometimes making notes or a table can help to clarify.

The question is asking about percent, so it is easy and fast to skim the passage for a percent sign.

The first percent sign is in the second paragraph, 30 - 35%. Write this in the margin. Next, see what this percent refers to, which is the mortality rate. Write "mortality" next to 30 - 35%. Now, working backwards, see what the 30 - 35% mortality rate refers to. At the beginning of that sentence, is Variola Major.

| 30 - 35% | Mortality | V. Major |

Now we have a clear understanding of what the passage is saying, which we have retrieved quickly and easily, and now hopefully we will not get confused by the different choices.

Choices A and B can be eliminated right away. Choice C looks correct. Check choice D quickly, and confirm that it is incorrect. Choice C is the correct answer.

22. B
Choices A and B are opposites. Is Variola Minor more or less severe, with more or fewer pox, and more or less scarring? The other two choices, "no pox" and "no treatment" can be eliminated quickly. Either choice A or B are going to be wrong.

Make a quick table like this:

Major - more serious - scars, blindness
Minor - milder

The passage does not mention scarring from Variola minor, but we can infer that it is milder. Looking at the options, choice A is clearly talking about Variola major, and we can infer that choice B is talking about Variola minor and is the correct answer. We can confirm our inference from the text.

Also note the words, 'major' and 'minor.' Which gives a clue concerning severity, and the elimination of choice A.

23. A
Choices A and B are not exactly opposite, but very close and designed to confuse if you do not read them properly. How many people die from the virus? Between 30 and 35%? Or between 35 and 60%? Scan the text with these numbers in mind.

This question is asking about a percent figures, so quickly scan the passage for a percent sign, which first appears in the second paragraph. Working back, confirm that the percent figures is related to mortality, which it is.

Strategy 7 - Look for Differences.

Look at two choices that appear to be correct and examine them carefully.

24. B
Choices A, B and C are very similar and designed to confuse and distract someone who does not look carefully at the text. What is astraphobia exactly? This is a definition question for an unusual word, astraphobia. Scan the text for "astraphobia." Choice B is correct.

25. C
Choices A, B and C are similar and designed to confuse, or tempt a stressed or careless test-taker into making a quick and incorrect choice. Checking the passage, in the first paragraph, lightning occurs in thunderstorms, volcanic eruptions and in dust storms, so choice C is correct.

26. C
All four answers are similar and designed to confuse. Seeing how similar the choices are, it is very important to be clear on the exact definition. Scan the text quickly for the word "fulgurites." From the first paragraph, fulgurites are formed when lightning is "... hot enough to fuse silica sand into glass channels ..." so the correct answer, and the option that answers the question best, is choice C, "Made of silica turned into glass."

Strategy 8 - Context clues.

Look at the sentences and the context to determine the best option. Sometimes, the answer may be located right in the passage or question.

27. B
You do not have to know the exact meaning - just enough to answer the question. The phrase is used in the passage, "After the Moon, it is the brightest natural object in the night sky, reaching an apparent magnitude of −4.6" where Venus is compared to the brightness of the moon, so the apparent magnitude must have something to do with brightness, which is enough information to answer the question. Notice also,

how the choices are opposites. Choice A and B are opposites as are choices C and D.

28. A
The exact meaning is not necessary, you only need only enough information to answer the question. The passage where this phrase is used is, "Because Venus is an inferior planet from Earth, it never appears to venture far from the Sun: its elongation reaches a maximum of 47.8°." Elongation in this sentence is something connected with distance from the sun, but also something to do with Earth. Choice C can be eliminated right away, and since one choice is wrong, Choice D, All of the Above, can also be eliminated. Choice A is the most likely correct because it mentions, "as seen from earth."

29. A
Choices C and D can be eliminated right away. No mention is made of size or people, so choices C and D are also incorrect. Terrestrial has many similar meanings, but choice A is the best. From the passage, "Venus is one of the four solar terrestrial planets, meaning that, like the Earth, it is a rocky body."

Note that choice B is a grammatical error and can be eliminated right away. The question is, "Terrestrial planets are," and choice B is, "Have people on them."

This is a great strategy, looking for grammatical errors and eliminating, and what you might expect to see on a test that a professor has made themselves. However, most standardized tests are generated by computer, and proofed by many different people who have considerable expertise in correcting this type of easy question. Keep this in mind because it is an easy elimination, but don't expect to see this type of thing on a standardized test.

30. A
This is a bit of a trick question and designed to confuse, as it requires an additional step of logical reasoning. Referring to the text, Venus is the *second* closest planet to the sun so there must be one planet that is closer. Planets closer to the sun will rotate the sun faster, so the answer must be choice A.

Strategy 9 - Try out every option for word meaning questions.

For definition questions, try out all the options - one option will fit better than the rest. As you go through the options, use Strategy 5 - Elimination, to eliminate obviously incorrect choices as you go.

31. B
The answer is taken directly from the passage. Notice that choices A and B are opposites, so one of them will be incorrect. Look in the text carefully for the exact definition. If you are uncertain, make a table in the margin.

Scan the passage looking for the word you are asked to define. Large or unusual words generally stand out and can be located quickly. Once you have found the position in the passage of the word using quick reading scanning techniques, then focus on the sentence and read carefully.

32. B
The sentences talking about the jet stream and monsoons are next to one another. Trying each definition, and comparing to the text, only choice B fits. If you are uncertain, copy the information from the passage into a table.

The question is, what is the relationship between monsoons and the jet stream.

Scan the passage for "jet stream" and "monsoon."

Tropical cyclones	Jet stream
Monsoons and thunderstorms	Different processes

33. D
Referring to the passage, and trying each definition choice, choice D is the only answer that makes sense referring to the text.

34. A
The passage from the text is, "Because the Earth's axis is tilted relative to its orbital plane, sunlight is incident at different angles at different times of the year." Substituting all the

choices given into this sentence, slanted, choice A, is the only sensible answer. Here is what substitutions look like:

    a. In June the Northern Hemisphere is *slanted* towards the sun...

    b. In June the Northern Hemisphere is *rotating* towards the sun...

    c. In June the Northern Hemisphere is *connected to* towards the sun...

    d. In June the Northern Hemisphere is *bent* towards the sun...

Choice A is the only one that makes sense.

Strategy 10 - You have to work for it! Check carefully for supporting details.

All answers can be found by carefully reading the text. The questions paraphrase the text found in the passage.

35. C
The passage has a lot of details so read carefully and stay clear.

36. B
The choices are designed to confuse. Check the text for the exact definition and do not be distracted by other choices.

37. A
Here is a quick tip. On choice A, the word hypovolemic is used. This is an unusual word and specific medical vocabulary. None of the other choices uses any specific vocabulary like this, so it is very likely to be the right answer. You can quickly scan the text for this word to confirm. Scanning the text for an unusual word is easy and fast, and one of the most powerful techniques for this type of question.

38. C
Scan the text for Zaire.

Strategy 11 - Look at the big picture

Details can be tricky when dealing with main idea and summary questions, but do not let the details distract you. Look at the big picture instead of the smaller parts to determine the right answer.

39. D
The passage says in 2005 it was found there are 3 fruit bat species most suspected of carrying the virus. The details (3 species, fruit bats and 2005) do not matter. Only the fact that bats are suspected.

40. B
The relevant passage is, "Of 24 plant species and 19 vertebrate species experimentally inoculated with Ebola virus, only bats became infected." The inference is that these plant and animal species cannot be infected, (i.e. carry and transmit the disease) so choice B is correct.

41. A
The relevant passage is, "Bats are also known to be the reservoirs for several related viruses including Nipah virus, Hendra virus and Lyssaviruses."

Strategy 12 - Make the best choice based on the information given.

42. D
Choices B and C are incorrect by the passage, "In the early stages, Ebola may not be highly contagious." Choice A is not mentioned, leaving choice D.

43. B
The passage does not say anything about the information in choices A and D. Choice C is irrelevant to the question.

44. A
Choices B and C are not mentioned in the passage. Choice D is a good possibility, however, choice A covers choice D and is referred to in the passage.

45. B
Choice A is incorrect. Choices C and D are not mentioned.

Practice Questions Answer Sheet

1. A B C D
2. A B C D
3. A B C D
4. A B C D
5. A B C D
6. A B C D
7. A B C D
8. A B C D
9. A B C D
10. A B C D
11. A B C D
12. A B C D
13. A B C D
14. A B C D
15. A B C D
16. A B C D
17. A B C D
18. A B C D
19. A B C D
20. A B C D
21. A B C D
22. A B C D
23. A B C D
24. A B C D
25. A B C D

Reading Comprehension Practice Questions

Questions 1 - 4 refer to the following passage.

Passage 1: "If You Have Allergies, You're Not Alone"

People who experience allergies might joke that their immune systems have let them down or are seriously lacking. Truthfully though, people who experience allergic reactions or allergy symptoms during certain times of the year have heightened immune systems that are, "better" than those of people who have perfectly healthy but less militant immune systems.

Still, when a person has an allergic reaction, they are having an adverse reaction to a substance that is considered normal to most people. Mild allergic reactions usually have symptoms like itching, runny nose, red eyes, or bumps or discoloration of the skin. More serious allergic reactions, such as those to animal and insect poisons or certain foods, may result in the closing of the throat, swelling of the eyes, low blood pressure, an inability to breathe, and can even be fatal.

Different treatments help different allergies, and which one a person uses depends on the nature and severity of the allergy. It is recommended to patients with severe allergies to take extra precautions, such as carrying an EpiPen, which treats anaphylactic shock and may prevent death, always in order for the remedy to be readily available and more effective. When an allergy is not so severe, treatments may be used just relieve a person of uncomfortable symptoms. Over the counter allergy medicines treat milder symptoms, and can be bought at any grocery store and used in moderation to help people with allergies live normally.

There are many tests available to assess whether a person has allergies or what they may be allergic to, and advances in these tests and the medicine used to treat patients continues to improve. Despite this fact, allergies still affect many people throughout the year or even every day. Medicines used to treat allergies have side effects of their own, and it is difficult to bring the body into balance with the use of medicine. Regardless, many of those who live with allergies are grateful for what is available and find it useful in maintaining their lifestyles.

1. According to this passage, it can be understood that the word "militant" belongs in a group with the words:

    a. sickly, ailing, faint
    b. strength, power, vigor
    c. active, fighting, warring
    d. worn, tired, breaking down

2. The author says that "medicines used to treat allergies have side effects of their own" to

    a. point out that doctors aren't very good at diagnosing and treating allergies

    b. argue that because of the large number of people with allergies, a cure will never be found

    c. explain that allergy medicines aren't cures and some compromise must be made

    d. argue that more wholesome remedies should be researched and medicines banned

3. It can be inferred that _____ recommend that some people with allergies carry medicine with them.

    a. the author
    b. doctors
    c. the makers of EpiPen
    d. people with allergies

4. The author has written this passage to

    a. inform readers on symptoms of allergies so people with allergies can get help

    b. persuade readers to be proud of having allergies

    c. inform readers on different remedies so people with allergies receive the right help

    d. describe different types of allergies, their symptoms, and their remedies

Questions 5 - 8 refer to the following passage.

Passage 2: "When a Poet Longs to Mourn, He Writes an Elegy"

Poems are an expressive, especially emotional, form of writing. They have been present in literature virtually from the time civilizations invented the written word. Poets often portrayed as moody, secluded, and even troubled, but this is because poets are introspective and feel deeply about the current events and cultural norms they are surrounded with. Poets often produce the most telling literature, giving insight into the society and mind-set they come from. This can be done in many forms.

The oldest types of poems often include many stanzas, may or may not rhyme, and are more about telling a story than experimenting with language or words. The most common types of ancient poetry are epics, which are usually extremely long stories that follow a hero through his journey, or elegies, which are often solemn in tone and used to mourn or lament something or someone. The Mesopotamians are often said to have invented the written word, and their literature is among the oldest in the world, including the epic poem titled "Epic of Gilgamesh." Similar in style and length to "Gilgamesh" is "Beowulf," an elegy poem written in Old English and set in Scandinavia. These poems are often used by professors as the earliest examples of literature.

The importance of poetry was revived in the Renaissance. At

this time, Europeans discovered the style and beauty of ancient Greek arts, and poetry was among those. Shakespeare is the most well-known poet of the time, and he used poetry not only to write poems but also to write plays for the theater. The most popular forms of poetry during the Renaissance included villanelles (a nineteen-line poem with two rhymes throughout), sonnets, as well as the epic. Poets during this time focused on style and form, and developed very specific rules and outlines for how an exceptional poem should be written.

As often happens in the arts, modern poets have rejected the constricting rules of Renaissance poets, and free form poems are much more popular. Some modern poems would read just like stories if they weren't arranged into lines and stanzas. It is difficult to tell which poems and poets will be the most important, because works of art often become more famous in hindsight, after the poet has died and society can look at itself without being in the moment. Modern poetry continues to develop, and will no doubt continue to change as values, thought, and writing continue to change.

Poems can be among the most enlightening and uplifting texts for a person to read if they are looking to connect with the past, connect with other people, or try to gain an understanding of what is happening in their time.

5. In summary, the author has written this passage

> a. as a foreword that will introduce a poem in a book or magazine
>
> b. because she loves poetry and wants more people to like it
>
> c. to give a brief history of poems
>
> d. to convince students to write poems

6. The author organizes the paragraphs mainly by

   a. moving chronologically, explaining which types of poetry were common in that time

   b. talking about new types of poems each paragraph and explaining them a little

   c. focusing on one poet or group of people and the poems they wrote

   d. explaining older types of poetry so she can talk about modern poetry

7. The author's claim that poetry has been around "virtually from the time civilizations invented the written word" is supported by the detail that

   a. Beowulf is written in Old English, which is not really in use any longer

   b. epic poems told stories about heroes

   c. the Renaissance poets tried to copy Greek poets

   d. the Mesopotamians are credited with both inventing the word and writing "Epic of Gilgamesh"

8. According to the passage, it can be understood that the word "telling" means

   a. speaking
   b. significant
   c. soothing
   d. wordy

Questions 9 - 12 refer to the following passage.

Passage 3: "Winged Victory of Samothrace: the Statue of the Gods"

Students who read about the "Winged Victory of Samothrace" probably won't be able to picture what this statue looks like. However, almost anyone who knows a little about statues will recognize it when they see it: it is the statue of a winged woman who does not have arms or a head. Even the most famous pieces of art may be recognized by sight but not by name.

This iconic statue is of the Greek goddess Nike, who represented victory and was called Victoria by the Romans. The statue is sometimes called the "Nike of Samothrace." She was often displayed in Greek art as driving a chariot, and her speed or efficiency with the chariot may be what her wings symbolize. It is said that the statue was created around 200 BCE to celebrate a battle that was won at sea. Archaeologists and art historians believe the statue may have originally been part of a temple or other building, even one of the most important temples, Megaloi Theoi, just as many statues were used during that time.

"Winged Victory" does indeed appear to have had arms and a head when it was originally created, and it is unclear why they were removed or lost. Indeed, they have never been discovered, even with all the excavation that has taken place. Many speculate that one of her arms was raised and put to her mouth, as though she was shouting or calling out, which is consistent with the idea of her as a war figure. If the missing pieces were ever to be found, they might give Greek and art historians more of an idea of what Nike represented or how the statue was used. Learning about pieces of art through details like these can help students remember time frames or locations, as well as learn about the people who occupied them.

9. The author's title says the statue is "of the Gods" because

    a. the statue is very beautiful and even a god would find it beautiful

    b. the statue is of a Greek goddess, and gods were of primary importance to the Greek

    c. Nike lead the gods into war

    d. the statues were used at the temple of the gods and so it belonged to them

10. The third paragraph states that

    a. the statue is related to war and was probably broken apart by foreign soldiers

    b. the arms and head of the statue cannot be found because all the excavation has taken place

    c. speculations have been made about what the entire statue looked like and what it symbolized

    d. the statue has no arms or head because the sculptor lost them

11. The author's main purpose in writing this passage is to

    a. demonstrate that art and culture are related and one can teach us about the other

    b. persuade readers to become archeologists and find the missing pieces of the statue

    c. teach readers about the Greek goddess Nike

    d. to teach readers the name of a statue they probably recognize

12. The author specifies the indirect audience as "students" because

    a. it is probably a student who is taking this test

    b. most young people don't know much about art yet and most young people are students

    c. students read more than people who are not students

    d. the passage is based on a discussion of what we can learn about culture from art

Questions 13 - 16 refer to the following passage.

Passage 4: "Ways Characters Communicate in Theater"

Playwrights give their characters voices in a way that gives depth and added meaning to what happens on stage during their play. There are different types of speech in scripts that allow characters to talk with themselves, with other characters, and even with the audience.

It is very unique to theater that characters may talk "to themselves." When characters do this, the speech they give is called a soliloquy. Soliloquies are usually poetic, introspective, moving, and can tell audience members about the feelings, motivations, or suspicions of an individual character without that character having to reveal them to other characters on stage. "To be or not to be" is a famous soliloquy given by Hamlet as he considers difficult but important themes, such as life and death.

The most common type of communication in plays is when one character is speaking to another or a group of other characters. This is generally called dialogue, but can also be called monologue if one character speaks without being interrupted for a long time. It is not necessarily the most important type of communication, but it is the most common because the plot of the play cannot really progress without it.

Lastly, and most unique to theater (although it has been used somewhat in film) is when a character speaks directly to the audience. This is called an aside, and scripts usually specifically direct actors to do this. Asides are usually comical, an inside joke between the character and the audience, and very short. The actor will usually face the audience when delivering them, even if it's for a moment, so the audience can recognize this move as an aside.

All three of these types of communication are important to the art of theater, and have been perfected by famous playwrights like Shakespeare. Understanding these types of communication can help an audience member grasp what is artful about the script and action of a play.

13. According to the passage, characters in plays communicate to

    a. move the plot forward

    b. show the private thoughts and feelings of one character

    c. make the audience laugh

    d. add beauty and artistry to the play

14. When Hamlet delivers "To be or not to be," he can most likely be described as

    a. solitary

    b. thoughtful

    c. dramatic

    d. hopeless

15. The author uses parentheses to punctuate "although it has been used somewhat in film"

    a. to show that films are less important

    b. instead of using commas so that the sentence is not interrupted

    c. because parenthesis help separate details that are not as important

    d. to show that films are not as artistic

16. It can be understood that by the phrase "give their characters voices," the author means that

    a. playwrights are generous

    b. playwrights are changing the sound or meaning of characters' voices to fit what they had in mind

    c. dialogue is important in creating characters

    d. playwrights may be the parent of one of their actors and literally give them their voice

Questions 17 - 20 refer to the following passage.

Passage 5: "Women and Advertising"

Only in the last few generations have media messages been so widespread and so readily seen, heard, and read by so many people. Advertising is an important part of both selling and buying anything from soap to cereal to jeans. For whatever reason, more consumers are women than are men. Media message are subtle but powerful, and more attention has been paid lately to how these message affect women.

Of all the products that women buy, makeup, clothes, and other stylistic or cosmetic products are among the most popular. This means that companies focus their advertising on women, promising them that their product will make her feel, look, or smell better than the next company's product will. This competition has resulted in advertising that is more and more ideal and less and less possible for everyday women. However, because women do look to these ideals and the products they represent as how they can potentially become, many women have developed unhealthy attitudes about themselves when they have failed to become those ideals.

In recent years, more companies have tried to change advertisements to be healthier for women. This includes featuring models of more sizes and addressing a huge outcry against unfair tools such as airbrushing and photo editing. There is debate about what the right balance between real and ideal is, because fashion is also considered art and some changes are made to purposefully elevate fashionable products and signify that they are creative, innovative, and the work of individual people. Artists want their freedom protected as much as women do, and advertising agencies are often caught in the middle.

Some claim that the companies who make these changes are not doing enough. Many people worry that there are still not enough models of different sizes and different ethnicities. Some people claim that companies use this healthier type of advertisement not for the good of women, but because they would like to sell products to the women who are looking for these kinds of messages. This is also a hard balance to find: companies do need to make money, and women do need to feel respected.

While the focus of this change has been on women, advertising can also affect men, and this change will hopefully be a lesson on media for all consumers.

17. The second paragraph states that advertising focuses on women

    a. to shape what the ideal should be

    b. because women buy makeup

    c. because women are easily persuaded

    d. because of the types of products that women buy

18. According to the passage, fashion artists and female consumers are at odds because

    a. there is a debate going on and disagreement drives people apart

    b. both of them are trying to protect their freedom to do something

    c. artists want to elevate their products above the reach of women

    d. women are creative, innovative, individual people

19. The author uses the phrase "for whatever reason" in this passage to

    a. keep the focus of the paragraph on media messages and not on the differences between men and women

    b. show that the reason for this is unimportant

    c. argue that it is stupid that more women are consumers than men

    d. show that he or she is tired of talking about why media messages are important

20. This passage suggests that

   a. advertising companies are still working on making their messages better

   b. all advertising companies seek to be more approachable for women

   c. women are only buying from companies that respect them

   d. artists could stop producing fashionable products if they feel bullied

Questions 21 - 24 refer to the following passage.

Passage 6: "FDR, the Treaty of Versailles, and the Fourteen Points"

At the conclusion of World War I, both who had won the war and those who were forced to admit defeat welcomed the end of the war and anticipated that a peace treaty would be signed. The American president, Franklin Roosevelt, played an important part in proposing what the agreements should be and did so through his Fourteen Points.

World War I had begun in 1914 when an Austrian archduke was assassinated, leading to a domino effect that pulled the world's most powerful countries into war on a large scale. The war catalyzed the creation and use of deadly weapons that had not previously existed, resulting in a great loss of soldiers on both sides of the fighting. More than 9 million soldiers were killed.

The United States agreed to enter the war right before it ended, and they believed that its decision to become finally involved brought on the end of the war. FDR made it very clear that the U.S. was entering the war for moral reasons and had an agenda focused on world peace. The Fourteen Points were individual goals and ideas (focused on peace, free trade, open communication, and self reliance) that FDR wanted the power nations to strive for now that the war had concluded.

He was optimistic and had many ideas about what could be accomplished through and during the post-war peace. However, FDR's fourteen points were poorly received when he presented them to the leaders of other world powers, many of whom wanted only to help their own countries and to punish the Germans for fueling the war, and they fell by the wayside. World War II was imminent, for Germany lost everything.

Some historians believe that the other leaders who participated in the Treaty of Versailles weren't receptive to the Fourteen Points because World War I was fought almost entirely on European soil, and the United States lost much less than did the other powers. FDR was in a unique position to help determine the fate of the war, but doing it on his own terms did not help accomplish his goals. This is only one historical example of how the United State has tried to use its power as an important country, but found itself limited because of geological or ideological factors.

21. The main idea of this passage is that

> a. World War I was unfair because no fighting took place in America
>
> b. World War II happened because of the Treaty of Versailles
>
> c. the power the United States has to help other countries also prevents it from helping other countries
>
> d. Franklin Roosevelt was one of the United States' smartest presidents

22. According to the second paragraph, World War I started because

> a. an archduke was assassinated
>
> b. weapons that were more deadly had been developed
>
> c. a domino effect of allies agreeing to help
>
> d. the world's most powerful countries were large

23. The author includes the detail that 9 million soldiers were killed

    a. to demonstrate why European leaders were hesitant to accept peace

    b. to show the reader the dangers of deadly weapons

    c. to make the reader think about which countries lost the most soldiers

    d. to demonstrate why World War II was imminent

24. According to this passage, it can be understood that the word catalyzed means

    a. analyzed

    b. sped up

    c. invented

    d. funded

Answer Key

Passage 1: "If You Have Allergies, You're Not Alone"

1. C
This question tests the reader's vocabulary skills. The uses of the negatives "but" and "less," especially right next to each other, may confuse readers into answering with choices A or D, which list words that are antonyms of "militant." Readers may also be confused by the comparison of healthy people with what is being described as an overly healthy person--both people are good, but the reader may look for which one is "worse" in the comparison, and therefore stray toward the antonyms. One key to understanding the meaning of "militant" if the reader is unfamiliar with it is to look at the root of the word; readers can then easily associate it with "military" and gain a sense of what the word signifies: defense (especially considered that the immune system defends the body). Choice C is correct over choice B because "militant" is an adjective, just as the words in C are, whereas the words in B are nouns.

2. C
This question tests the reader's understanding of function within writing. The other choices are details included surrounding the quoted text, and may therefore confuse the reader. A somewhat contradicts what is said earlier in the paragraph, which is that tests and treatments are improving, and probably doctors are along with them, but the paragraph doesn't actually mention doctors, and the subject of the question is the medicine. Choice B may seem correct to readers who aren't careful to understand that, while the author does mention the large number of people affected, the author is touching on the realities of living with allergies rather about the likelihood of curing all allergies. Similarly, while the author does mention the "balance" of the body, which is easily associated with "wholesome," the author is not really making an argument and especially is not making an extreme statement that allergy medicines should be outlawed. Again, because the article's tone is on living with allergies, choice C is an appropriate choice that fits with the title and content of the text.

3. B
This question tests the reader's inference skills. The text does not state who is doing the recommending, but the use of the "patients," as well as the general context of the passage, lends itself to the logical partner, "doctors," B. The author does mention the recommendation but doesn't present it as her own (i.e. "I recommend that"), so A may be eliminated. It may seem plausible that people with allergies (D) may recommend medicines or products to other people with allergies, but the text does not necessarily support this interaction taking place. Choice C may be selected because the EpiPen is specifically mentioned, but the use of the phrase "such as" when it is introduced is not limiting enough to assume the recommendation is coming from its creators.

4. D
This question tests the reader's global understanding of the text. Choice D includes the main topics of the three body paragraphs, and isn't too focused on a specific aspect or quote from the text, as the other questions are, giving a skewed summary of what the author intended. The reader may be drawn to Choice B because of the title of the passage and the use of words like "better," but the message of the passage is larger and more general than this.

Passage 2: "When a Poet Longs to Mourn, He Writes an Elegy"

5. C
This question tests the reader's summarization skills. The use of the word "actually" in describing what kind of people poets are, as well as other moments like this, may lead readers to selecting choice B or D, but the author is more information than trying to persuade readers. The author gives no indication that she loves poetry (B) or that people, students specifically (D), should write poems. Choice A is incorrect because the style and content of this paragraph do not match those of a foreword; forewords usually focus on the history or ideas of a specific poem to introduce it more fully and help it stand out against other poems. The author here focuses on several poems and gives broad statements. Instead, she tells a kind

of story about poems, giving three very broad time periods in which to discuss them, thereby giving a brief history of poetry, as choice C states.

6. A
This question tests the reader's summarization skills. Key words in the topic sentences of each of the paragraphs ("oldest," "Renaissance," "modern") should give the reader an idea that the author is moving chronologically. The opening and closing sentence-paragraphs are broad and talk generally. Choice B seems reasonable, but epic poems are mentioned in two paragraphs, eliminating the idea that only new types of poems are used in each paragraph. Choice C is also easily eliminated because the author clearly mentions several different poets, groups of people, and poems. Choice D also seems reasonable, considering that the author does move from older forms of poetry to newer forms, but use of "so (that)" makes this statement false, for the author gives no indication that she is rushing (the paragraphs are about the same size) or that she prefers modern poetry.

7. D
This question tests the reader's attention to detail. The key word is "invented"--it ties together the Mesopotamians, who invented the written word, and the fact that they, as the inventors, also invented and used poetry. The other selections focus on other details mentioned in the passage, such as that the Renaissance's admiration of the Greeks (C) and that Beowulf is in Old English (A). Choice B may seem like an attractive answer because it is unlike the others and because the idea of heroes seems rooted in ancient and early civilizations.

8. B
This question tests the reader's vocabulary and contextualization skills. "Telling" is not an unusual word, but it may be used here in a way that is not familiar to readers, as an adjective rather than a verb in gerund form. Choice A may seem like the obvious answer to a reader looking for a verb to match the use they are familiar with. If the reader understands that the word is being used as an adjective and that choice A is a ploy, they may opt to select choice D, "wordy," but it does not make sense in context. Choice C can be easily eliminated, and doesn't have any connection to the paragraph or passage.

"Significant" (B) does make sense contextually, especially relative to the phrase "give insight" used later in the sentence.

Passage 3: "Winged Victory of Samothrace: the Statue of the Gods"

9. B
This question tests the reader's summarization skills. Choice A is a very broad statement that may or may not be true, and seems to be in context, but has nothing to do with the passage. The author does mention that the statue was probably used on a temple dedicated to the Greek gods (D), but in no way discusses or argues for the gods' attitude toward or claim on these temples or its faucets. Nike does indeed lead the gods into a war (the Titan war), as choice C suggests, but this is not mentioned by the passage and students who know this may be drawn to this answer but have not done a close enough analysis of the text that is actually in the passage. Choice B is appropriately expository, and connects the titular emphasis to the idea that the Greek gods are very important to Greek culture.

10. C
This question tests the reader's summarization skills. The test for question choice C is pulled straight from the paragraph, but is not word-for-word, so it may seem too obvious to be the right answer. The passage does talk about Nike being the goddess of war, as choice A states, but the third paragraph only touches on it and it is an inference that soldiers destroyed the statue, when this question is asking specifically for what the third paragraph actually stated. Choice B is also straight from the text, with a minor but key change: the inclusion of the words "all" and "never" are too limiting and the passage does not suggest that these limits exist. If a reader selects choice D, they are also making an inference that is misguided for this type of question. The paragraph does state that the arms and head are "lost" but does not suggest who lost them.

11. A
This question tests the reader's ability to recognize function in writing. Choice B can be eliminated based on the purpose of the passage, which is expository and not persuasive. The author may or may not feel this way, but the passage does

not show evidence of being argumentative for that purpose. Choices C and D are both details found in the text, but neither of them encompasses the entire message of the passage, which has an overall message of learning about culture from art and making guesses about how the two are related, as suggested by choice A.

12. D
This question tests the reader's ability to understand function within writing. Most of the possible selections are very general statements which may or may not be true. It probably is a student who is taking the test on which this question is featured (A), but the author makes no address to the test taker and is not talking to the audience in terms of the test. Likewise, it may also be true that students read more than adults (C), mandated by schools and grades, but the focus on the verb "read" in the first sentence is too narrow and misses the larger purpose of the passage; the same could be said for selection B. While all the statements could be true, choice D is the most germane, and infers the purpose of the passage without making assumptions that could be incorrect.

Passage 4: "Ways Characters Communicate in Theater"

13. D
This question tests the reader's summarization skills. The question is asking very generally about the message of the passage, and the title, "Ways Characters Communicate in Theater," is one indication of that. The other choices A, B, and C are all directly from the text, and therefore readers may be inclined to select one of them, but are too specific to encapsulate the entirety of the passage and its message.

14. B
The paragraph on soliloquies mentions "To be or not to be," and it is from the context of that paragraph that readers may understand that because "To be or not to be" is a soliloquy, Hamlet will be introspective, or thoughtful, while delivering it. It is true that actors deliver soliloquies alone, and may be "solitary" (A), but "thoughtful" (B) is more true to the overall idea of the paragraph. Readers may choose C because drama and theater can be used interchangeably and the passage mentions that soliloquies are unique to theater (and therefore

drama), but this answer is not specific enough to the paragraph in question. Readers may pick up on the theme of life and death and Hamlet's true intentions and select that he is "hopeless" (D), but those themes are not discussed either by this paragraph or passage, as a close textual reading and analysis confirms.

15. C
This question tests the reader's grammatical skills. Choice B seems logical, but parenthesis are actually considered to be a stronger break in a sentence than commas are, and along this line of thinking, actually disrupt the sentence more. Choices A and D make comparisons between theater and film that are simply not made in the passage, and may or may not be true. This detail does clarify the statement that asides are most unique to theater by adding that it is not completely unique to theater, which may have been why the author didn't chose not to delete it and instead used parentheses to designate the detail's importance (C).

16. C
This question tests the reader's vocabulary and contextualization skills. Choice A may or may not be true, but focuses on the wrong function of the word "give" and ignores the rest of the sentence, which is more relevant to what the passage is discussing. CHoices B and D may also be selected if the reader depends too literally on the word "give," failing to grasp the more abstract function of the word that is the focus of choice C, which also properly acknowledges the entirety of the passage and its meaning.

Passage 5: "Women and Advertising"

17. D
This question tests the reader's summarization skills. The other choices A, B, and C focus on portions of the second paragraph that are too narrow and do not relate to the specific portion of text in question. The complexity of the sentence may mislead students into selecting one of these answers, but rearranging or restating the sentence will lead the reader to the correct answer. In addition, choice A makes an assumption that may or may not be true about the intentions of the company, choice B focuses on one product rather than

the idea of the products, and choice C makes an assumption about women that may or may not be true and is not supported by the text.

18. B
This question tests reader's attention to detail. If a reader selects A, he or she may have picked up on the use of the word "debate" and assumed, very logically, that the two are at odds because they are fighting; however, this is simply not supported in the text. Choice C also uses very specific quotes from the text, but it rearranges them and gives them false meaning. The artists want to elevate their creations above the creations of other artists, thereby showing that they are "creative" and "innovative." Similarly, choice D takes phrases straight from the texts and rearranges and confuses them. The artists are described as wanting to be "creative, innovative, individual people," not the women.

19. A
This question tests reader's vocabulary and summarization skills. This phrase, used by the author, may seem flippant and dismissive if readers focus on the word "whatever" and misinterpret it as a popular, colloquial terms. In this way, the choices B and C may mislead the reader to selecting one of them by including the terms "unimportant" and "stupid," respectively. Choice D is a similar misreading, but doesn't make sense when the phrase is at the beginning of the passage and the entire passage is on media messages. Choice A is literarily and contextually appropriate, and the reader can understand that the author would like to keep the introduction focused on the topic the passage is going to discuss.

20. A
This question tests a reader's inference skills. The extreme use of the word "all" in choice B suggests that every single advertising company are working to be approachable, and while this is not only unlikely, the text specifically states that "more" companies have done this, signifying that they have not all participated, even if it's a possibility that they may some day. The use of the limiting word "only" in choice C lends that answer similar problems; women are still buying from companies who do not care about this message, or those companies would not be in business, and the passage speci-

fies that "many" women are worried about media messages, but not all. Readers may find choice D logical, especially if they are looking to make an inference, and while this may be a possibility, the passage does not suggest or discuss this happening. Choice A is correct based on specifically because of the relation between "still working" in the answer and "will hopefully" and the extensive discussion on companies struggles, which come only with progress, in the text.

Passage 6: "FDR, the Treaty of Versailles, and the Fourteen Points"

21. C
This question tests the reader's summarization skills. The entire passage is leading up to the idea that the president of the US may not have had grounds to assert his Fourteen Points when other countries had lost so much. Choice A is pretty directly inferred by the text, but it does not adequately summarize what the entire passage is trying to communicate. Choice B may also be inferred by the passage when it says that the war is "imminent," but it does not represent the entire message, either. The passage does seem to be in praise of FDR, or at least in respect of him, but it does not in any way claim that he is the smartest president, nor does this represent the many other points included. Choice C is then the obvious answer, and most directly relates to the closing sentences which it rewords.

22. C
This question tests the reader's attention to detail. The passage does state that choices A and B are true, and while those statements are in proximity to the explanation for why the war started, they are not the actual reason given. Choice D is a mix up of words used in the passage, which says that the largest powers were in play but not that this fact somehow started the war. The passage does make a direct statement that a domino effect started the war, supporting choice C as the correct answer.

23. A
This question tests the reader's understanding of functions in writing. Throughout the passage, it states that leaders of other nations were hesitant to accept generous or peaceful terms

because of the grievances of the war, and the great loss of life was chief among these. While the passage does touch on the devastation of deadly weapons (B), the use of this raw, emotional fact serves a much larger purpose, and the focus of the passage is not the weapons. While readers may indeed consider who lost the most soldiers (C) when so many countries were involved and the inequalities of loss are mentioned in the passage, there is no discussion of this in the passage. Choice D is related to A, but choice A is more direct and relates more to the passage.

24. B
This question tests the reader's vocabulary skills. Choice A may seem appealing to readers because it is phonetically similar to "catalyzed," but the two are not related in any other way. Choice C makes sense in context, but if plugged into the sentence creates a redundancy that doesn't make sense. Choice D does also not make sense contextually, even if the reader may consider that funds were needed to create more weaponry, especially if it was advanced.

English Grammar Multiple-Choice

How to Answer English Grammar Multiple-Choice - Verb Tense

This tutorial is designed to help you answer English Grammar multiple-choice questions as well as a very quick refresher on verb tenses. It is assumed that you have some familiarity with the verb tenses covered here. If you find these questions difficulty or do not understand the tense construction, we recommend you seek out additional instruction.

Tenses Covered

1. Past Progressive
2. Present Perfect
3. Present Perfect Progressive
4. Present Progressive
5. Simple Future
6. Simple Future – "Going to" Form
7. Past Perfect Progressive
8. Future Perfect Progressive
9. Future Perfect
10. Future Progressive
11. Past Perfect

1. The Past Progressive Tense

How to Recognize This Tense

He *was running* very fast when he fell.

They *were drinking* coffee when he arrived.

About the Past Progressive Tense

This tense is used to speak of an action that was in progress in the past when another event occurred.

The action was unfolding at a point in the past.

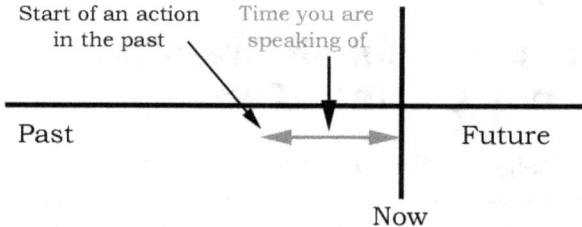

Past Progressive Tense Construction

This tense is formed by using the past tense of the verb "to be" plus the present participle of the main verb.

Sample Question

Bill _____ lunch when we arrived.

    a. will eat
    b. is eating
    c. eats
    d. was eating

How to Answer This Type of Question

1. First examine the question for clues about the time frame.

The sentence ends with "when we arrived," so we know the time frame is a point ("when") in the past (arrived).

The correct answer will refer to an ongoing action at a point of time in the past.

2. Examine the choices and eliminate any obviously incorrect answers.

Choice A is the future tense so we can eliminate.

Choice B is the present continuous so we can eliminate.

Choice C is present tense so we can eliminate.

Choice D refers to an action that takes place at a point of time in the past ("was eating").

2. The Present Perfect Tense

How to Recognize This Tense

I *have had* enough to eat.

We *have been* to Paris many times.

I *have known* him for five years.

I *have been* coming here since I was a child.

About the Present Perfect Tense

This tense expresses the idea that something happened (or didn't happen) at an unspecific time in the past until the present. The action happened at an unspecified time in the past. (If there is a specific time mentioned, the simple past tense is used.) It can be used for repeated action, accomplishments, changes over time and uncompleted action.

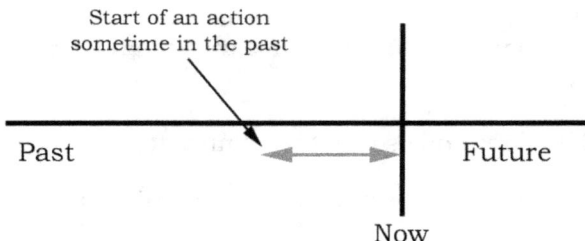

Present Perfect Tense Construction

It is also used with "for" and "since."

This tense is formed by using the present tense of the verb "to have" plus the past participle of the main verb.

Sample Question

I _____ these birds many times.

    a. am seeing
    b. will saw
    c. have seen
    d. have saw

How to Answer This Type of Question

1. First examine the question for clues about the time frame.

"Many times" tells us that the action is repeated and in the past.

2. Examine the choices and eliminate any obviously incorrect answers.

Choice A, "am seeing" is incorrect because it is a continuing action, i.e. in the present; it also doesn't use a form of 'have'.

Choice B is grammatically incorrect.

Choice C tells of something that has happened in the past and is now over. Best choice so far.

Choice D is grammatically incorrect.

3. The Present Perfect Progressive Tense

How to Recognize This Tense

We *have been seeing* a lot of rainy days.

I *have been reading* some very good books.

About the Present Perfect Progressive Tense

This tense expresses the idea that something happened (or didn't happen) in the relatively recent past, but <u>the action is not finished.</u> It is used to express the duration of the action.

NOTE: The present perfect speaks of an action that happened sometime in the past, but this action is finished. In the present perfect progressive tense, the action that started in the past is still going on.

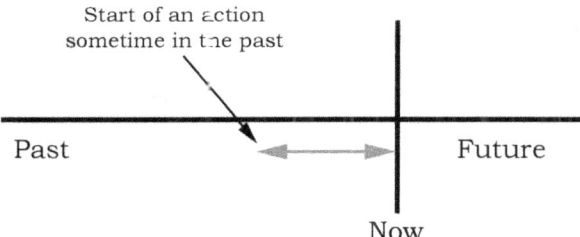

Present Perfect Progressive Tense Construction

This tense is formed by using the present tense of the verb "to have," plus "been," plus the present participle of the main verb.

Sample Question

Bill _____ there for two hours.

    a. sits
    b. sitting
    c. has been sitting
    d. will sat

How to Answer This Type of Question

1. First examine the question for clues about the time frame.

"For two hours" tells us that the action, "sits," is continuous up to now, and may continue into the future.

Note this sentence could also be the simple past tense,

Bill sat there for two hours.

Or the future tense,

Bill will sit there for two hours.

However, these are not among the options.

2. Examine the choices and eliminate any obviously incorrect answers.

Choice A is incorrect because it is the present tense.
Choice B is incorrect because it is the present continuous.
Choice C is correct. "Has been sitting" expresses a continuous action in the past that isn't finished.
Choice D is grammatically incorrect.

4. The Present Progressive Tense

How to Recognize This Tense

We *are having* a delicious lunch.

They *are driving* much too fast.

About the Present Progressive Tense

This tense is used to express what the action is <u>right now</u>. The action started in the recent past, and is continuing into the future.

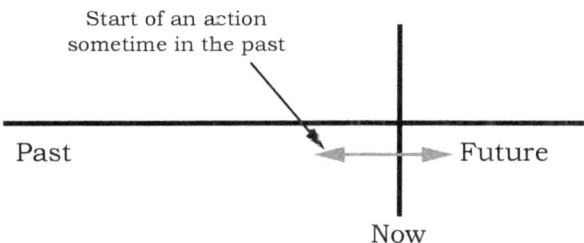

Present Perfect Tense Construction

The Present Progressive Tense is formed by using the present tense of "to be" plus the present participle of the main verb.

Sample Question

She _____ very hard these days.

    a. works
    b. is working
    c. will work
    d. worked

How to Answer This Type of Question

1. First examine the question for clues about the time frame.

The end of the sentence includes "these days" which tell us the action started in the past, continues into the present, and may continue into the future.

2. Examine the choices and eliminate any obviously incorrect answers.

Choice A, the simple present is incorrect.
Choice B, "is working" is correct.
Check the other two choices just to be sure. Choice C is future tense, and choice D is past tense, so they can be eliminated.
The correct answer is choice B.

5. The Simple Future Tense

How to Recognize This Tense

I *will see* you tomorrow.
We *will drive* the car.

About the Simple Future Tense

This tense shows that the action will happen some time in the future.

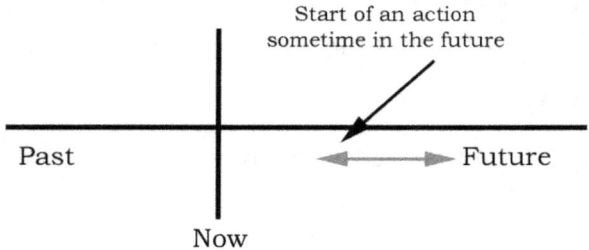

Simple Future Tense Construction

The tense is formed by using "will" plus the root form of the verb. (The root form of the verb is the infinitive without "to." Examples: read, swim.)

Sample Question

We _____ to Paris next year.

    a. went
    b. had been
    c. will go
    d. go

How to Answer This Type of Question

1. First examine the question for clues about the time frame.

The last two words of the sentence, "next year," clearly identify this sentence as referring to the future.

2. Examine the choices and eliminate any obviously incorrect answers.

Choice A is the past tense and can be eliminated.

Choice B is the past perfect tense and can be eliminated.

Choice D is the simple present and can be eliminated.

Choice C is the only one left and is the correct simple future tense.

6. The Simple Future Tense – The "Going to" Form

How to Recognize This Tense

I *am going to* see you tomorrow.

We *are going to* drive the car.

About the Simple Future Tense

This form of the future tense is used to show the intention of doing something in the future. (This is the strict grammatical meaning, but in daily speech, it is often used interchangeably with the simple future tense, the "will" form.)

The tense is formed by using the present conditional tense of "to go," plus the infinitive of the verb.

Sample Question

I _____ shopping in an hour.

    a. go
    b. have gone
    c. am going to go
    d. went

How to Answer This Type of Question

1. First examine the question for clues about the time frame.

"In an hour" clearly identifies the action as taking place in the future.

2. Examine the choices and eliminate any obviously incorrect answers.
Choice A is the simple present tense and can be eliminated.

Choice B is the past perfect and can be eliminated.

Choice C is the correct answer.

Choice D is the past tense and can be eliminated.

7. The Past Perfect Progressive Tense

How to Recognize This Tense

I *had been sleeping* for an hour when you phoned.

We *had been eating* our dinner when they all came into the dining room.

About the Past Perfect Progressive Tense

This tense is used to show that the action had been going on for a period of time in the past when another action, also in the past, occurred.

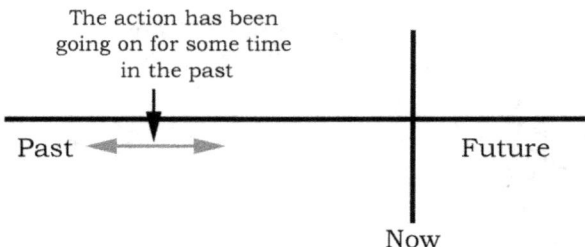

Past Perfect Tense Construction

The tense is formed by using the past perfect tense of the verb "to be" plus the present participle of the main verb.

Sample Question

How long _____ you _____ when I saw you?

    a. are _____ running
    b. had _____ running
    c. had _____ been running
    d. was _____ running

How to Answer This Type of Question

1. First examine the question for clues about the time frame.

"When I saw" tells us the sentence happened at a point of time ("when") in the past ("saw").

2. Examine the choices and eliminate any obviously incorrect answers.

Choice A, "are running" is incorrect and can be eliminated.

Choice B, "Had ___ running" is grammatically incorrect and can be eliminated.

Choice C is correct.

Choice D is grammatically incorrect so the answer is Choice C.

8. Future Perfect Progressive Tense

How to Recognize This Tense

I *will have been working* here for two years in March.

I *will have been driving* for four hours when I get there, so I will be tired.

About the Future Perfect Progressive Tense

This tense is used to show that the action continues up to a point of time in the future.

Future Prefect Progressive Tense Construction

This tense is formed by using the future perfect tense of "to be" plus the present participle of the main verb.

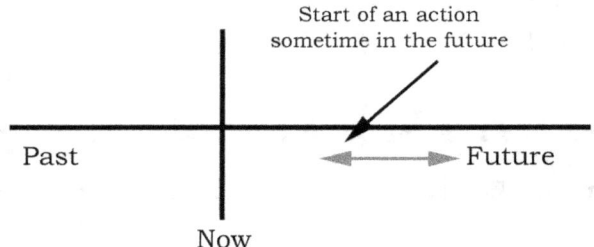

Sample Question

_____ you _____ all the time I am gone?

    a. have _____ been working
    b. will _____ have been working
    c. are _____ worked
    d. will _____ worked

How to Answer This Type of Question

1. First examine the question for clues about the time frame.

"All the time I am gone" refers to an action in the future ("time I am gone") and the action is progressive ("all the time"). The progressive action means the correct choice will be a verb tense that ends in "ing."

2. Examine the choices and eliminate any obviously incorrect answers.

Choice A, the past perfect, refers to a past continuous event and is also grammatically incorrect in the sentence, so choice A can be eliminated.

Choice B looks correct because it refers to an action will be going on for a period of time in the future.

Examine choices C and D just to be sure. Both choices are grammatically incorrect and can be eliminated. Choice B is the correct answer.

9. The Future Perfect Tense

How to Recognize This Tense

By next November, I *will have received* my promotion.

By the time he gets home, she is going *to have cleaned* the entire house.

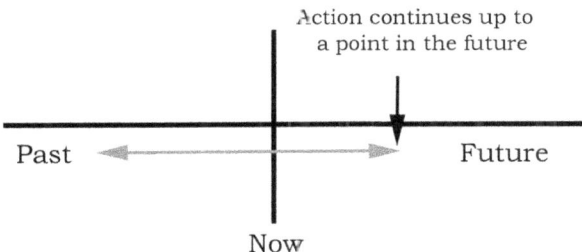

About the Future Perfect Tense

The future perfect tense expresses action in the future before another action in the future. This is the past in the future. For example:

He *will have prepared* dinner when she arrives.

Future Perfect Tense Construction

This tense is formed by "will + have + past participle."

Sample Question

They _____ their seats before the game begins.

    a. will have find
    b. will find
    c. will have found
    d. found

How to Answer This Type of Question

1. First examine the question for clues about the time frame.

This question could be several different tenses. The only clue about the time frame is "before the game begins," which refers to a specific point of time.

We know it isn't in the past, because "begins" is incorrect for the past tense. Similarly with the present. So the question is about something that happens in the future, before another event in the future.

2. Examine the choices and eliminate any obviously incorrect answers.

Choice A can be eliminated as incorrect.
Choice B looks good, so mark it and check the others before making a final decision.
Choice C is the past perfect and can be eliminated because the time frame is incorrect.
Choice D is the simple past tense and can be eliminated for the same reason.

10. Future Progressive Tense

How to Recognize This Tense

The teams *will be playing* soccer when we arrive.

At 3:45 the soccer fans *will be waiting* for the game to start at 4:00 o'clock

At 3:45 the soccer players *will be preparing* to play at 4:00 o'clock

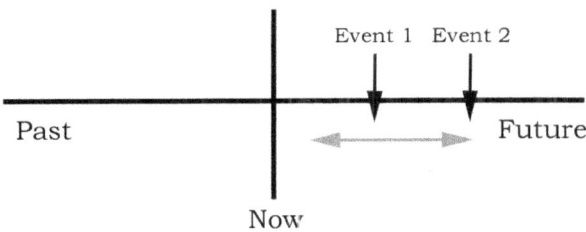

About the Future Progressive Tense

The future progressive tense talks about a continuing action in the future.

Future Progressive Tense Construction

will+ be + (root form) + ing = will be playing

Sample Question

Many excited fans _____ a bus to see the game at 4:00.

    a. catch
    b. catching
    c. have been catching
    d. will be catching

How to Answer This Type of Question

1. First examine the question for clues about the time frame.

"At 4:00," tells us the sentence is either in the past OR in the future.

2. Examine the choices and eliminate any obviously incorrect answers.

From the time frame of the sentence, the answer will be past or future tense.

Choice A is the present tense and can be eliminated.
Choice B is the present continuous tense and can be eliminated.
Choice C is the past perfect continuous and can be eliminated.
Choice D is the only one left. Quickly examining the tense, it is future progressive and is correct in the sentence.

11. The Past Perfect Tense

How to Recognize This Tense

The party *had* just *started* when the coach arrived.

We *had waited* for twenty minutes when the bus finally came.

About the Past Perfect

The past perfect tense talks about two events that happened in the past and establishes which event happened first.

Another example is, "We had eaten when he arrived."

The two events are "eat" and "he arrived." From the sentence above the past perfect tense tells us the first event, "eat" happened before the second event, "he arrived."

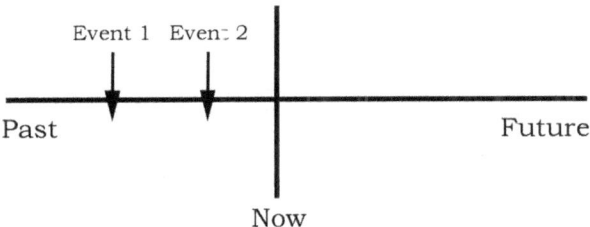

I had already eaten when my friends arrived.

Past Perfect Tense Construction

The past perfect is formed by "have" plus the past participle.

Sample Question

It was time to go home after they _____ the game.

    a. will win

    b. win

    c. had won

    d. wins

How to Answer This Type of Question

1. First examine the question for clues about the time frame.

"Was" tells us the sentence happened in the past. Also notice there are two events, "go home" and "after the game."

2. Examine the choices and eliminate any obviously incorrect answers.

Choice A is the future tense and can be eliminated. Choice B is the simple present and can be eliminated. Choice C is the past perfect and orders the two events in the past. Choice D is the present tense and incorrect and can be eliminated, so choice C is the correct answer.

Common English Usage Mistakes - A Quick Review

Like some parts of English grammar, usage is definitely going to be on the exam and there isn't any tricky strategies or shortcuts to help you get through this section.
Here is a quick review of common usage mistakes.

1. May and Might

'May' can act as a principle verb, which can express permission or possibility.
Examples:

Lets wait, the meeting may have started.
May I begin now?

'May' can act as an auxiliary verb, which an expresses a purpose or wish

Examples:

May you find favour in the sight of your employer.

May your wishes come true.
People go to school so that they may be educated.

The past tense of may is might.

Examples:

I asked if I might begin

'Might' can be used to signify a weak or slim possibility or polite suggestion.

Examples:

You might find him in his office, but I doubt it.
You might offer to help if you want to.

2. Lie and Lay

The verb lay should always take an object. The three forms of the verb lay are: laid, lay and laid.

The verb lie (recline) should not take any object. The three forms of the verb lie are: lay, lie and lain.

Examples:

Lay on the bed.
The tables were laid by the students.
Let the little kid lie.
The patient lay on the table

The dog has lain there for 30 minutes.

Note: The verb lie can also mean "to tell a falsehood." This verb can appear in three forms: lied, lie, and lied. This is different from the verb lie (recline) mentioned above.

Examples:

The accused is fond of telling lies.
Did she lie?

3. Would and should

The past tense of shall is 'should', and so "should" generally follows the same principles as "shall."

The past tense of will is "would," and so "would" generally follows the same principles as "will."

The two verbs 'would and should' can be correctly used interchangeably to signify obligation. The two verbs also have some unique uses too. Should is used in three persons to signify obligation.

Examples:

I should go after work.

People should do exercises everyday.
You should be generous.

"Would" is specially used in any of the three persons, to signify willingness, determination and habitual action.

Examples:

They would go for a test run every Saturday.
They would not ignore their duties.
She would try to be punctual.

4. Principle and Auxiliary Verbs

Two principle verbs can be used along with one auxiliary verb as long as the auxiliary verb form suits the two principle verbs.

Examples:

A number of people have been employed and some promoted.

A new tree has been planted and the old has been cut down.

Again note the difference in the verb form.

5. Can and Could

A. Can is used to express capacity or ability.

Examples:

I can complete the assignment today
He can meet up with his target.

B. Can is also used to express permission.

Examples:

Yes, you can begin

In the sentence below, "can" was used to mean the same thing as "may." However, the difference is that the word "can" is used for negative or interrogative sentences, while "may" is used in affirmative sentences to express possibility.

Examples:

They may be correct. Positive sentence - use may.
Can this statement be correct? A question using "can."
It cannot be correct. Negative sentence using "can."

The past tense of can is could. It can serve as a principle verb when it is used to express its own meaning.

Examples:

In spite of the difficulty of the test, he could still perform well. "Could" here is used to express ability.

6. Ought

The verb ought should normally be followed by the word to.

Examples:

I *ought to* close shop now.

The verb 'ought' can be used to express:

A. Desirability

You ought to wash your hands before eating. It is desirable to wash your hands.

B. Probability

She ought to be on her way back by now. She is probably on her way.

C. Moral obligation or duty

The government ought to protect the oppressed. It is the government's duty to protect the oppressed.

7. Raise and Rise

Rise
The verb rise means to go up, or to ascend.
The verb rise can appear in three forms, rose, rise, and risen.
The verb should not take an object.

Examples:

The bird rose very slowly.
The trees rise above the house.
My aunt has risen in her career.

Raise
The verb raise means to increase, to lift up.
The verb raise can appear in three forms, raised, raise and raised.

Examples:

He raised his hand.
The workers requested a raise.
Do not raise that subject.

8. Past Tense and Past Participle

Pay attention to the proper use these verbs: sing, show, ring, awake, fly, flow, begin, hang and sink.

Mistakes usually occur when using the past participle and past tense of these verbs as they are often mixed up.

Each of these verbs can appear in three forms:

Sing, Sang, Sung.
Show, Showed, Showed/Shown.
Ring, Rang, Rung.
Awake, awoke, awaken
Fly, Flew, Flown.

Flow, Flowed, Flowed.
Begin, Began, Begun.
Hang, Hanged, Hanged (a criminal)
Hang, Hung, Hung (a picture)
Sink, Sank, Sunk.

Examples:

The stranger rang the door bell. (simple past tense)
I have rung the door bell already. (past participle - an action completed in the past)

The stone sank in the river. (simple past tense)
The stone had already sunk. (past participle - an action completed in the past)

The meeting began at 4:00.
The meeting has begun.

9. Shall and Will

When speaking informally, the two can be used interchangeably. In formal writing, they must be used correctly.

"Will" is used in the second or third person, while "shall" is used in the first person. Both verbs are used to express a time or even in the future.

Examples:

I shall, We shall (First Person)
You will (Second Person)
They will (Third Person)

This principle however reverses when the verbs are to be used to express threats, determination, command, willingness, promise or compulsion. In these instances, will is now used in first person and shall in the second and third person.

Examples:

I will be there next week, no matter what.
This is a promise, so the first person "I" takes "will."
You shall ensure that the work is completed.
This is a command, so the second person "you" takes "shall."

I will try to make payments as promised.
This is a promise, so the first person "I" takes "will."

They shall have arrived by the end of the day.
This is a determination, so the third person "they" takes shall.

Note
A. The two verbs, shall and will should not occur twice in the same sentence when the same future is being referred to

Example:

I shall arrive early if my driver is here on time.

B. Will should not be used in the first person when questions are being asked

Examples:

Shall I go ?
Shall we go?

Subject Verb Agreement

Verbs in any sentence must agree with the subject of the sentence both in person and number. Problems usually occur when the verb doesn't correspond with the right subject or the verb fails to match the noun close to it.

Unfortunately, there is no easy way around these principles - no tricky strategy or easy rule. You just have to memorize them.

Here is a quick review:

The verb to be, present (past)

Person	Singular	Plural
First	I am (was)	we are (were)
Second	you are (were)	you are (were)
Third	he, she, it is (was)	they are (were)

The verb to have, present (past)

Person	Singular	Plural
First	I have (had)	we have (had)
Second	you have (had)	you have (had)
Third	he, she, it has (had)	they have (had)

Regular verbs, e.g. to walk, present (past)

Person	Singular	Plural
First	I walk (walked)	we walk (walked)
Second	you walk (walked)	you walk (walked)
Third	he, she, it walks (walked)	they work (walked)

1. Every and Each

When nouns are qualified by "every" or "each," they take a singular verb even if they are joined by 'and'

Examples:

Each mother and daughter *was* a given separate test.

Every teacher and student *was* properly welcomed.

2. Plural Nouns

Nouns like measles, tongs, trousers, riches, scissors etc. are all plural.

Examples:

The trousers *are* dirty.
My scissors *have* gone missing.
The tongs *are* on the table.

3. With and As Well

Two subjects linked with "with" or "as well" should have a verb that matches the first subject.

Examples:

The pencil, with the papers and equipment, *is* on the desk.
David as well as Louis is coming.

4. Plural Nouns

The following nouns take a singular verb:

> politics, mathematics, innings, news, advice, summons, furniture, information, poetry, machinery, vacation, scenery

Examples:

The machinery *is* difficult to assemble
The furniture *has* been delivered
The scenery *was* beautiful

5. Single Entities

A proper noun in plural form that refers to a single entity requires a singular verb. This is a complicated way of saying; some things appear to be plural, but are really singular, or some nouns refer to a collection of things but the collection is really singular.

Examples:

The United Nations Organization *is* the decision maker in the matter.

Here the "United Nations Organization" is really only one "thing" or noun, but is made up of many "nations."

The book, "The Seven Virgins" *was* not available in the library.

Here there is only one book, although the title of the book is plural.

6. Specific Amounts are always singular

A plural noun that refers to a specific amount or quantity that is considered as a whole (dozen, hundred, score etc) requires a singular verb.

Examples:

60 minutes *is* quite a long time.
Here "60 minutes" is considered a whole, and therefore one item (singular noun).

The first million is the most difficult.

7. Either, Neither and Each are always singular

The verb is always singular when used with: either, each, neither, every one and many.

Examples:

Either of the boys *is* lying.
Each of the employees *has* been well compensated
Many a police officer *has* been found to be courageous
Every one of the teachers *is* responsible

8. Linking with Either, Or, and Neither match the second subject

Two subjects linked by "either," "or," "nor" or "neither" should have a verb that matches the second subject.

Examples:

Neither David nor Paul *will* be coming.
Either Mary or Tina *is* paying.

Note
If one of the subjects linked by "either," "or," "nor" or "neither" is in plural form, then the verb should also be in plural, and the verb should be close to the plural subject.

Examples:
Neither the mother *nor* her kids *have* eaten.
Either Mary *or* her *friends are* paying.

9. Collective Nouns are Plural

Some collective nouns such as poultry, gentry, cattle, vermin etc. are considered plural and require a plural verb.

Examples:

The *poultry are* sick.
The *cattle are* well fed.

Note
Collective nouns involving people can work with both plural

and singular verbs.

Examples:

Nigerians are known to be hard working
Europeans live in Africa

10. Nouns that are Singular and Plural

Nouns like deer, sheep, swine, salmon etc. can be singular or plural and require the same verb form.

Examples:

The swine is feeding. (singular)
The swine are feeding. (plural)

The salmon is on the table. (singular)
The salmon are running upstream. (plural)

11. Collective Nouns are Singular

Collective nouns such as Army, Jury, Assembly, Committee, Team etc should carry a singular verb when they subscribe to one idea. If the ideas or views are more than one, then the verb used should be plural.

Examples:

The committee is in agreement in their decision.

The committee were in disagreement in their decision.
The jury has agreed on a verdict.

The jury were unable to agree on a verdict.

12. Subjects links by "and" are plural.

Two subjects linked by "and" always require a plural verb

Examples:

David and John are students.

Note
If the subjects linked by "and" are used as one phrase, or constitute one idea, then the verb must be singular

The color of his socks and shoe is black.
Here "socks and shoe" are two nouns, however the subject is "color" which is singular.

English Grammar and Usage Answer Sheet

1. A B C D
2. A B C D
3. A B C D
4. A B C D
5. A B C D
6. A B C D
7. A B C D
8. A B C D
9. A B C D
10. A B C D
11. A B C D
12. A B C D
13. A B C D
14. A B C D
15. A B C D
16. A B C D
17. A B C D
18. A B C D
19. A B C D
20. A B C D
21. A B C D
22. A B C D
23. A B C D
24. A B C D
25. A B C D
26. A B C D
27. A B C D
28. A B C D
29. A B C D
30. A B C D
31. A B C D
32. A B C D
33. A B C D
34. A B C D
35. A B C D
36. A B C D
37. A B C D
38. A B C D
39. A B C D
40. A B C D
41. A B C D
42. A B C D
43. A B C D
44. A B C D
45. A B C D
46. A B C D
47. A B C D
48. A B C D
49. A B C D
50. A B C D
51. A B C D
52. A B C D
53. A B C D
54. A B C D
55. A B C D
56. A B C D
57. A B C D
58. A B C D
59. A B C D
60. A B C D

English Grammar Practice Questions

1. Choose the sentence with the correct grammar.

    a. The man was asked to come with his daughter and her test results.

    b. The man was asked to come with her daughter and her test results.

    c. The man was asked to come with her daughter and our test results.

    d. None of the above.

2. Choose the sentence with the correct grammar.

    a. Every doctor must come with his stethoscope

    b. Every doctor must come with their stethoscope

    c. Every doctor must come with our stethoscope

    d. None of the above.

3. Choose the sentence with the correct grammar.

    a. Each of them have to be given a ticket.

    b. Each of them is to be given a ticket.

    c. Each of them are to be given a ticket.

    d. None of the above.

4. Choose the sentence with the correct grammar.

    a. The scenery were breathtaking.

    b. The scenery was breathtaking.

    c. Both of the above

    d. None of the above

5. Choose the sentence with the correct grammar.

    a. Neither the teacher nor the student is left in class.
    b. Neither the teacher nor the student are left in class.
    c. Both of the above.
    d. None of the above.

6. Choose the sentence with the proper usage.

    a. The meeting may have started.
    b. The meeting might have started.
    c. Both of the above.
    d. None of the above.

7. Choose the sentence with the proper usage.

    a. He can be correct
    b. He could be correct
    c. He may be correct
    d. None of the above

8. Choose the sentence with the correct grammar.

    a. The vermin are to be exterminated.
    b. The vermin is to be exterminated.
    c. The vermin was to be exterminated.
    d. None of the above.

9. Choose the sentence with the correct grammar.

    a. The salmon has been cooked.
    b. The salmon have been cooked.
    c. Both of the above.
    d. None of the above.

10. Choose the sentence with the correct grammar.

    a. Many of the students came with their lunch box.
    b. Many of the students came with our lunch box.
    c. Many of the students came with his or her lunch box.
    d. None of the above.

11. Choose the sentence with the correct grammar.

    a. The driver and the cleaner were to be sacked.
    b. The driver and the cleaner are to be sacked.
    c. The driver and the cleaner is to be sacked.
    d. None of the above.

12. Choose the sentence with the correct grammar.

    a. Here are the names of people whom you should contact.
    b. Here are the names of people who you should contact.
    c. Both of the above.
    d. None of the above.

13. Choose the sentence with the proper usage.

    a. Christians believe that their lord have raised.
    b. Christians believe that their lord have risen.
    c. Christians believe that their lord have raise.
    d. None of the above.

14. Choose the sentence with the proper usage.

    a. I will be at the office by 9 a. m.
    b. I shall be at the office by 9 a. m.
    c. Both of the above.
    d. None of the above.

15. Choose the sentence with the correct grammar.

    a. The army are interested in buying the property.
    b. The army is interested in buying the property.
    c. The army were interested in buying the property.
    d. None of the above.

16. Choose the sentence with the correct grammar.

    a. The poultry is sold off yesterday.
    b. The poultry were sold off yesterday.
    c. The poultry was sold off yesterday.
    d. None of the above.

17. Choose the sentence with the correct grammar.

    a. Mark and Peter have stopped to each other.
    b. Mark and Peter have stopped to one another.
    c. Both of the above.
    d. None of the above.

18. Choose the sentence with the correct grammar.

    a. The teacher asked everybody is to submit his assignment by 9 a.m.
    b. The teacher asked everybody is to submit our assignment by 9 a.m.
    c. The teacher asked everybody is to submit their assignment by 9 a.m.
    d. None of the above.

19. Choose the sentence with the proper usage.

    a. I will ensure that you receive the proper reward.
    b. I shall ensure that you receive the proper reward.
    c. Both of the above.
    d. None of the above.

20. Choose the sentence with the proper usage.

    a. He ought to be back by now.
    b. He ought be back by now.
    c. He ought come back by now.
    d. None of the above.

21. Choose the sentence with the correct grammar.

    a. The gentry were well taken off at the reception.
    b. The gentry was well taken off at the reception.
    c. The gentry are well taken off at the reception.
    d. None of the above.

22. Choose the sentence with the correct grammar.

    a. The deer are running for their lives.
    b. The deer is running for their lives.
    c. Both of the above.
    d. None of the above.

23. Choose the sentence with the correct grammar.

    a. His measles is getting better.
    b. His measles are getting better.
    c. Both of the above.
    d. None of the above.

24. Choose the sentence with the correct grammar.

    a. Each player gets a locker to keep their personal things.
    b. Each player gets a locker to keep his personal things.
    c. Each player gets a locker to keep our personal things.
    d. None of the above.

25. Choose the sentence with the proper usage.

    a. The tables were laid by the students.
    b. The tables were lay by the students.
    c. The tables were lie by the students.
    d. None of the above.

26. Choose the sentence with the correct grammar.

    a. The teachers and the student are standing in the hall.
    b. The teachers and the student is standing in the hall.
    c. Both of the above.
    d. None of the above.

27. Choose the sentence with the proper usage.

    a. Shall I give my speech now?
    b. Will I give my speech now?
    c. Both of the above.
    d. None of the above.

28. Choose the sentence with the correct grammar.

    a. Any girl that fails the test loses their admission.
    b. Any girl that fails the test loses our admission.
    c. Any girl that fails the test loses her admission.
    d. None of the above.

29. Choose the sentence with the proper usage.

    a. The dog has lay there for 30 minutes.
    b. The dog has lie there for 30 minutes.
    c. The dog has lain there for 30 minutes.
    d. None of the above.

30. Choose the sentence with the correct grammar.

   a. The sad news were delivered this morning.
   b. The sad news are delivered this morning.
   c. The sad news was delivered this morning.
   d. None of that above.

31. Choose the sentence with the proper usage.

   a. He told him to raised it up.
   b. He told him to raise it up.
   c. He told him to rise it up.
   d. None of the above.

32. Choose the sentence with the correct grammar.

   a. Neither of them came with their bicycle.
   b. Neither of them came with his bicycle.
   c. Neither of them came with our bicycle.
   d. None of the above.

33. Choose the sentence with the proper usage.

   a. A number of people have been employed and others promoted.
   b. A number of people have been sacked and others have been employed.
   c. A number of people sacked and others have been promoted.
   d. None of the above.

34. Choose the sentence with the correct grammar.

a. Politics were a dirty game.
b. Politics is a dirty game.
c. Politics are a dirty game.
d. None of the above.

35. Choose the sentence with the correct grammar.

a. The members of the team were asked to discuss with each other.
b. The members of the team were asked to discuss with one another.
c. Both of the above.
d. None of the above.

36. Choose the sentence with the correct grammar.

a. Their wages is been cut by half.
b. Their wages has been cut by half.
c. Their wages have been cut by half.
d. None of the above.

37. Choose the sentence with the proper usage.

a. In spite of the BAD weather yesterday, he can still attend the party.
b. In spite of the BAD weather yesterday, he could still attend the party.
c. In spite of the BAD weather yesterday, he may still attend the party.
d. None of the above.

38. Choose the sentence with the correct grammar.

a. The World Health Organization (WHO) were meeting by January.

b. The World Health Organization (WHO) are meeting by January.

c. The World Health Organization (WHO) is meeting by January.

d. None of the above.

39. Choose the sentence with the correct grammar.

a. Everyone was asked to raise their hand.

b. Everyone was asked to raise our hand.

c. Everyone was asked to raise her hand.

d. None of the above.

40. Choose the sentence with the proper usage.

a. They never and never will disobey the rules.

b. They never have and never will disobey the rules.

c. Both of the above.

d. None of the above.

41. Choose the sentence with the correct grammar.

a. Neither of them were coming along.

b. Neither of them is coming along.

c. Neither of them are coming along.

d. None of the above.

42. Choose the sentence with the correct grammar.

a. Everyone are to wear a black tie.

b. Everyone have to wear a black tie.

c. Everyone has to wear a black tie.

d. None of the above.

43. Choose the sentence with the proper usage.

   a. She was nodding her head, her hips are swaying.
   b. She was nodding her head, her hips is swaying.
   c. She was nodding her head, her hips were swaying.
   d. None of the above

44. Choose the sentence with the correct grammar.

   a. The broken furniture has been replaced.
   b. The broken furniture have been replaced.
   c. The broken furniture is been replaced.
   d. None of the above.

45. Choose the sentence with the correct grammar.

   a. Who would be giving the opening address?
   b. Whom will be giving the opening address?
   c. Both of the above.
   d. None of the above.

46. Choose the sentence with the correct grammar.

   a. 15 minutes is all the time you have to complete the test.
   b. 15 minutes are all the time you have to complete the test.
   c. Both of the above.
   d. None of the above.

47. Choose the sentence with the proper usage.

   a. They will have to retire when they reach 60 years of age.
   b. They shall have to retire when they reach 60 years of age.
   c. Both of the above.
   d. None of the above.

48. Choose the sentence with the correct grammar.

    a. The scissors are on the table
    b. The scissors is on the table
    c. Both of the above
    d. None of the above

49. Choose the sentence with the correct grammar.

    a. The new machinery were working at full capacity
    b. The new machinery are working at full capacity
    c. The new machinery is working at full capacity
    c. None of the above

50. Choose the sentence with the correct grammar.

    a. Either Paul or Mary is the thief
    b. Either Paul or Mary are the thief
    c. Either Paul or Mary were the thief
    d. None of the above

Answer Key

1. A
A pronoun should conform to its antecedent in gender, number and person

2. A
Words such as neither, each, many, either, every, everyone, everybody and any should take a singular pronoun.

3. B
Use a singular verb with either, each, neither, everyone and many.

4. B
Always use the singular verb form for nouns like politics, wages, mathematics, innings, news, advice, summons, furniture, information, poetry, machinery, vacation, scenery etc.

5. A
When two subjects are linked by "either," "or," "nor," or "neither," use a verb that matches the second subject.

6. A
The verb "may" is used to express possibility or permission. Might is the past tense of may. In casual conversation, may and might are often used interchangeably, however, although it is grammatically incorrect.

7. C
Although the CAN could be used to mean the same thing as the word MAY, the difference is that the word can is used for negative or interrogative sentences, while may is used in affirmative sentences to express possibility.

8. A
Use the plural verb form with collective nouns such as poultry, gentry, cattle, vermin etc.

9. C
Nouns like deer, sheep, swine, salmon etc can take a singular

or plural verb depending if they are used in their singular or plural form.

10. C
Words such as neither, each, many, either, every, everyone, everybody and any should take a singular pronoun.

11. B
Two subjects linked by "and" with the use of the article "the" affects the nature of the verb to be used and so a plural verb is required.

12. A
Use "whom" in the objective case, and use "who" a subjective case.

13. B
The verb rise ('to go up', 'to ascend.') can appear in three forms, rise, rose, and risen. The verb should not take an object.

14. B
"Will" is used in the second or third person (they, he, she and you), while "shall" is used in the first person (I and we). Both verbs are used to express futurity. In common usage and everyday conversation, however, they can be interchanged.

15. B
Use the singular verb form with collective nouns such as army, jury, assembly, committee, team etc. when they subscribe to one idea. If the ideas or views are more than one, use the plural form.

16. B
Use the plural verb form with collective nouns such as poultry, gentry, cattle, vermin etc.

17. A
When you use 'each other' it should be used for two things or people. When you use 'one another' it should be used for things and people above two

18. A
Words such as neither, each, many, either, every, everyone, everybody and any should take a singular pronoun.

19. B
"Shall" is used in the second or third person (they, he, she and you), while "will" is used in the first person (I and we) when they are used to express threats, determination, command, willingness, promise or compulsion.

20. A
The verb "ought" can be used to express desirability, duty and probability. The verb is usually followed by "to."

21. A
Use the plural verb form with collective nouns such as poultry, gentry, cattle, vermin etc.

22. A
Nouns like deer, sheep, swine, salmon etc can take a singular or plural verb depending if they are used in their singular or plural form.

23. B
Use a plural verb for nouns like measles, tongs, trousers, riches, scissors etc.

24. B
Words such as neither, each, many, either, every, everyone, everybody and any should take a singular pronoun.

25. A
The verb "lay" should always take an object. Here the subject is the table. The three forms of the verb lay are: lay, laid and laid. The sentence above is in past tense.

26. A
When two subjects are linked with "with" or "as well," use the verb form that matches the first subject.

27. A
"Will" is used in the second or third person (they, he, she and you), while "shall" is used in the first person (I and we) when

questions are asked.

28. C
Words such as neither, each, many, either, every, everyone, everybody and any should take a singular pronoun.

29. C
The verb lie (recline) should not take an object. The three forms of the verb lie are: 1 lie, lay and lain. The sentence above is in past tense.

30. C
Always use the singular verb form for nouns like politics, wages, mathematics, innings, news, advice, summons, furniture, information, poetry, machinery, vacation, scenery etc.

31. B
The verb raise ('to increase', 'to lift up.') can appear in three forms, raise, raised and raised.

32. B
Use a singular pronoun with words such as neither, each, many, either, every, everyone, everybody and any. Here we are assuming that the subject is male, and so use "his." The subject could be female, in which case we would use "her," however that is not a choice here.

33. B
Two principal verbs can be used along with one auxiliary verb as long as the auxiliary verb form suits the two principal verbs.

34. B
Always use the singular verb form for nouns like politics, wages, mathematics, innings, news, advice, summons, furniture, information, poetry, machinery, vacation, scenery etc.

35. B
When you use 'each other' it should be used for two things or people. When you use 'one another' it should be used for things and people above two.

36. C
Always use the singular verb form for nouns like politics, wages, mathematics, innings, news, advice, summons, furniture, information, poetry, machinery, vacation, scenery etc.

37. B
Use "could," the past tense of "can" to express ability or capacity.

38. C
Use a singular verb with a proper noun in plural form that refers to a single entity. Here the "The World Health Organization" is a single entity, although it is made up on many members.

39. C
Words such as neither, each, many, either, every, everyone, everybody and any should take a singular pronoun. Here we are assuming that the subject is female, and so use "her." The subject could be male, in which case we would use "his," however that is not one of the choices.

40. B
One principal verb can be used correctly with two auxiliary verbs as long as the form of principal verb used suits the two auxiliary verbs.

41. B
Use a singular verb with either, each, neither, everyone and many.

42. C
Use a singular verb with either, each, neither, everyone and many.

43. C
A verb can fit any of the two subjects in a compound sentence as long as the verb form agrees with that subject.

44. A
Always use the singular verb form for nouns like politics, wages, mathematics, innings, news, advice, summons, furniture, information, poetry, machinery, vacation, scenery

etc.

45. A
Use "whom" in the objective case, and use "who" a subjective case.

46. A
Use a singular verb with a plural noun that refers to a specific amount or quantity that is considered as a whole (dozen, hundred score etc).

47. A
Will is used in the second or third person (they, he, she and you), while shall is used in the first person (I and we). Both verbs are used to express futurity.

48. A
Use a plural verb for nouns like measles, tongs, trousers, riches, scissors etc.

49. C
Always use the singular verb form for nouns like politics, wages, mathematics, innings, news, advice, summons, furniture, information, poetry, machinery, vacation, scenery etc.

50. A
Use a singular verb with either, each, neither, everyone and many.

Basic Math Multiple-Choice Strategy

Math is the one section where you need to make sure that you understand the processes before you ever tackle it. That's because the time allowed on the math portion is typically so short that there's not much room for error. It's imperative that before the test day arrives, you've learned all the main formulas that will be used, and then created your own problems that utilize the formula and then solved them.

On the actual test day, use the "Plug-Check-Check" strategy. Here's how it goes.

Read the problem, but not the answers. You'll want to work the problem first and come up with your own answers. If you did the work right, you should find your answer among the options given.

If you need help with the problem, plug actual numbers into the variables given. You'll find it easier to work with numbers than it is to work with letters. For instance, if the question asks, "If Y - 4 is 2 more than Z, then Y + 5 is how much more than Z?" try selecting a value for Y. Let's take 6. Your question now becomes, "If 6 - 4 is 2 more than Z, then 6 plus 5 is how much more than Z?" Now your answer should be easier to work with.

Check the answer options to see if your answer matches one of those. If so, select it.

If no answer matches the one you got, re-check your math, but this time, use a different method. In math, it's common for there to be more than one way to solve a problem. As a simple example, if you multiplied 12 X 13, and did not get an answer that matches one of the answer options, you might try adding 13 together 12 different times and see if you get a good answer.

Math Multiple-Choice Strategy

The two strategies for working with basic math multiple-choice are Estimation and Elimination.

Math Strategy 1 - Estimation

Just like it sounds, try to estimate an approximate answer first. Then look at the choices.

Math Strategy 2 - Elimination

For every question, no matter what type, eliminating obviously incorrect answers narrows the possible choices. Elimination is probably the most powerful strategy for answering multiple-choice.

Here are a few basic math examples of how this works.

Solve 2/3 + 5/12

    a. 9/17
    b. 3/11
    c. 7/12
    d. 1 1/12

First Estimate. 2/3 is more than half and 5/12 is about half, so the answer is going to be very close to 1.

Next, Eliminate. Choice A is about 1/2 and can be eliminated, Choice B is very small, less than 1/2 and can be eliminated. Choice C is close to 1/2 and can be eliminated. Leaving only choice D, which is just over 1.

Work through the solution, a common denominator is needed, a number which both 3 and 12 will divide into.
2/3 = 8/12. So, 8+5/12 = 13/12 = 1 1/12
Choice D is correct.

Here is another example:

Solve 4/5 – 2/3

    a. 2/2
    b. 2/13
    c. 1
    d. 2/15

You can eliminate choice A, because it is 1 and since both of the numbers are close to one, the difference is going to be very small. You can eliminate choice C for the same reason.

Next, look at the denominators. Since 5 and 3 don't go into 13, you can eliminate Choice B as well.

That leaves choice D.

Checking the answer, the common denominator will be 15. So 12-10/15 = 2/15. Choice D is correct.

Fractions shortcut - Cancelling out.

In any operation with fractions, if the numerator of one fractions has a common multiple with the denominator of the other, you can cancel out. This saves time and simplifies the problem quickly, making it easier to manage.

Solve 2/15 ÷ 4/5

    a. 6/65
    b. 6/75
    c. 5/12
    d. 1/6

To divide fractions, we multiply the first fraction with the inverse of the second fraction. Therefore we have 2/15 x 5/4. The numerator of the first fraction, 2, shares a multiple with the denominator of the second fraction, 4, which is 2. These cancel out, which gives, 1/3 x 1/2 = 1/6

Cancelling Out solved the questions very quickly, but we can still use multiple-choice strategies to answer.

Choice B can be eliminated because 75 is too large a denominator. Choice C can be eliminated because 5 and 15 don't go in to 12.

Choice D is correct.

Decimal Multiple-Choice strategy and Shortcuts.

Multiplying decimals gives a very quick way to estimate and eliminate choices. Anytime that you multiply decimals, it is going to give an answer with the same number of decimal places as the combined operands.

So for example,

2.38 X 1.2 will produce a number with three places of decimal, which is 2.856.
Here are a few examples with step-by-step explanation:

Solve 2.06 x 1.2

    a. 24.82
    b. 2.482
    c. 24.72
    d. 2.472

This is a simple question, but even before you start calculating, you can eliminate several choices. When multiplying decimals, there will always be as many numbers behind the decimal place in the answer as the sum of the ones in the initial problem, so choices A and C can be eliminated.

The correct answer is D: 2.06 x 1.2 = 2.472

Solve 20.0 ÷ 2.5

    a. 12.05
    b. 9.25
    c. 8.3
    d. 8

First estimate the answer to be around 10, and eliminate choice A. And since it'd also be an even number, you can eliminate choices B and C, leaving only choice D.

The correct Answer is D: 20.0 ÷ 2.5 = 8

Answer Sheet

1. (A) (B) (C) (D) 11. (A) (B) (C) (D) 21. (A) (B) (C) (D)
2. (A) (B) (C) (D) 12. (A) (B) (C) (D) 22. (A) (B) (C) (D)
3. (A) (B) (C) (D) 13. (A) (B) (C) (D) 23. (A) (B) (C) (D)
4. (A) (B) (C) (D) 14. (A) (B) (C) (D) 24. (A) (B) (C) (D)
5. (A) (B) (C) (D) 15. (A) (B) (C) (D) 25. (A) (B) (C) (D)
6. (A) (B) (C) (D) 16. (A) (B) (C) (D)
7. (A) (B) (C) (D) 17. (A) (B) (C) (D)
8. (A) (B) (C) (D) 18. (A) (B) (C) (D)
9. (A) (B) (C) (D) 19. (A) (B) (C) (D)
10. (A) (B) (C) (D) 20. (A) (B) (C) (D)

Basic Math Strategy Practice Questions

1. Solve 1/4 + 11/16

    a. 9/16
    b. 1 1/16
    c. 11/16
    d. 15/16

2. Solve 7/11 + 3/11

    a. 6/11
    b. 9/11
    c. 10/11
    d. 4/11

3. Solve 5/9 + 2/9

    a. 6/11
    b. 1 3/7
    c. 7/18
    d. 7/9

4. Solve 3/12 + 11/12

    a. 6/12
    b. 1/6
    c. 1 1/6
    d. 1 3/12

5. Solve 13/16 – 1/4

    a. 1
    b. 12/12
    c. 9/16
    d. 7/16

6. Solve 17/23 – 15/23

    a. 2
    b. 1/11
    c. 2/13
    d. 2/23

7. Solve 13/15 – 7/15

    a. 3/5
    b. 7/15
    c. 2/5
    d. 6

8. 33/49 – 23/49

    a. 10/49
    b. 11/49
    c. 10
    d. 13/23

9. Solve 3/4 X 5/11

    a. 2/15
    b. 10/44
    c. 3/19
    d. 15/44

10. Solve 6/10 x 5/16

    a. 4/15
    b. 3/16
    c. 2 1/3
    d. 2/7

11. Solve 3/7 x 4/7

    a. 6/27
    b. 12/49
    c. 3/19
    d. 2/7

12. Solve 4/5 x 2/5

    a. 5/21
    b. 6/25
    c. 8/25
    d. 1 3/5

13. Solve 5/8 ÷ 2/3

    a. 15/16
    b. 10/24
    c. 5/12
    d. 1 2/5

14. Solve 11/20 ÷ 9/20

    a. 99/20
    b. 4 19/20
    c. 1 2/9
    d. 1 1/9

15. Solve 7.25 x 0.5

   a. 3.625
   b. 3.526
   c. 36.25
   d. 35.25

16. Solve 21.02 x 0.34

   a. 71.468
   b. 7.1468
   c. 7.48
   d. 714.68

17. Solve 3.4 ÷ 1.7

   a. 12.05
   b. 9.25
   c. 8.3
   d. 2

18. Solve 2.4 + 3.9

   a. 6.3
   b. 7.3
   c. 5.3
   d. 6.13

19. Solve 3.34 + 2.13

   a. 54.7
   b. 5.57
   c. 5.47
   d. 54.7

20. Solve 42.87 + 26.401

    a. 9.033
    b. 90.33
    c. 73.03
    d. 69.271

21. Solve 6.363 - 1.602

    a. 4.011
    b. 4.761
    c. 47.61
    d. 3.761

22. Solve 67.54 – 43.45

    a. 24.09
    b. 24.19
    c. 24.019
    d. 23.09

23. Convert 75% to decimal

    a. 0.0075
    b. 0.075
    c. 0.75
    d. 7.5

24. Convert 39% to decimal

    a. 0.309
    b. 0.039
    c. 3.9
    d. 0.39

25. What is 25% of 135?

    a. 33.75
    b. 25
    c. 60
    d. 45.35

Answer Key

1. D
Since 9 is less than 11, you can eliminate choice A because an addition problem means that the final number won't be less than one of the initial numbers in the problem. And since 11 is equal to 11, you can eliminate choice C, based on that the sum would be a higher number than the ones you started out with.

Narrowing it down between choice B and D. From the two numbers, you can see that something over a whole number is going to be too high, which just leaves choice D.

Do the calculations to confirm.
A common denominator is needed, a number which both 4 and 16 will divide into. So, $4+11/16 = 15/16$

2. C
Since 4, 6, and 9 are all less than the sum of 7 + 3, you can eliminate choice A, B, and D.

Do the calculations to confirm.
Since the denominators are the same, we can just add the numerators, so $7+3/11 = 10/11$

3. D
You can eliminate choices A and B right away, since 9 does not go in to 11 or 7, so even if you needed to find a common denominator, neither one of those would be what you were looking for.

9 does go into 18, but it would mean you'd have to multiply everything by 2, and that would be equal to more than 7 when you added the numerators together.

Do the calculations to confirm. Since the denominators are the same, we can just add the numerators, so $5+2/9 = 7/9$

4. C
Choice A can be eliminated because 11/12 by itself is more than one half. Choice B can be eliminated because it is so

close to being 0, that 11/12 almost being a whole number means it cannot be 1/6.

Do the calculations to confirm.
Since the denominators are the same, we can just add the numerators, so 3+11/12 = 14/12 = 1 2/12 = 1 1/6

5. C
Choices A and B can both be eliminated because that are 1 and the difference of two fractions is not going to be 1.

Do the calculations to confirm.
A common denominator' is needed, number which both 16 and 4 will divide into. So 13-4/16 = 9/16

6. D
Choice A can be eliminated because 2 is a whole number, which would not be the difference between two subtracted fractions. Choices B and C can be eliminated since neither 11 or 13 go into 23.

Do the calculations to confirm.
Since the denominators are the same, subtract the numerators, so 17-15/23 = 2/23

7. C
You can eliminate choice D because it is a whole number. Since choice B is the same as one of the fractions in the problem, you can eliminate that, since subtracting it is not going to equal a number in the problem.

Do the calculations to confirm.
Since the denominators are the same, subtract the numerators, so 13-7/15 = 6/15 = 2/5

8. A
Choice C can be eliminated as it is a whole number. Choice D can be eliminated because 23 does not go evenly in to 49.

Do the calculations to confirm.
Since the denominators are the same, subtract the numerators, so 33-23/49 = 10/49

9. D
Since 15 and 19 are not common denominators with 4 or 11, choices A and C can be eliminated.

Do the calculations to confirm.
Since there are no common numerators and denominators to cancel out, multiply the numerators and then the denominators. So 3 x 5/4 x 1 = 15/44

10. B
Choice C can be eliminated because multiplying fractions does not give whole numbers. 15 and 7 are not common denominators with 10 or 16, so choices A and D can be eliminated as well.

Do the calculations to confirm.
Since there are common numerators and denominators to cancel out, 6/10 x 5/16 to get 6/2 x 1/16 = 3/2 x 1/8, and multiply numerators and denominators to get 3/16

11. B
Choice D can be eliminated because 2 is less than the product of 3 and 4. Since 7 doesn't go in to 27 or 19, choices A and C can be eliminated.

Do the calculations to confirm.
Since there are no common numerators and denominators to cancel out, we simply multiply the numerators and then the denominators. So 3 x 4/7 x 7 = 12/49

12. C
Since there are no common numerators and denominators to cancel out, we simply multiply the numerators and then the denominators. So 4 x 2/5 x 5 = 8/25

Since multiplying fractions doesn't come out as whole numbers, choice D can be eliminated. Since 5 does not divide evenly into 21, choice A can be eliminated.

13. A
Choice D can be eliminated because it is a number greater than 1. Since dividing fractions is just flipping one and multiplying by the other, choice C can be eliminated since 5 as the

numerator is too small. Since you have to flip the second fraction, choice B can be eliminated as well, as that's just multiplying straight across.

Do the calculations to confirm.
To divide fractions, we multiply the first fraction with the inverse of the second fraction. Therefore 5/8 x 3/2 = 15/16

14. C
Choice A can be eliminated because 99 is the produce of 11 and 9, which would not be multiplied in this problem. Choice B can be eliminated because 4 is too high of a number.

Do the calculations to confirm.
11/20 x 20/9 = 11/1 x 1/9 = 11/9 = 1 2/9

15. A
When multiplying decimals, there should be as many numbers behind the decimal place in the answer, as the sum of the ones in the initial problem, choices C and D can be eliminated. Since it's a multiple of 5, the last number would be 5 and not 6, eliminating choice B.

Do the calculations to confirm.
 7.25 x 0.5 = 3.625

16. B
When multiplying decimals, there should be as many numbers behind the decimal place in the answer, as the sum of the ones in the initial problem, choices A C, and D can be eliminated.

Do the calculations to confirm.
21.02 x 0.34 = 7.1468

17. D
Since the estimate of this would be around 1.5, choices A, B, and C are all too high to be the answer.

Do the calculations to confirm.
3.4 ÷ 1.7 = 2

18. A
A quick estimate of equation would be about 6. Choice B is too high and can be eliminated. Choice C is too low, and can be eliminated.

Do the calculations to confirm.
2.4 + 3.9 = 6.3

19. C
A quick estimate would be about 5, which would make choices A and D too high to be the answer.

Do the calculations to confirm.
3.34 + 2.13 = 5.47

20. D
Choice A is too small to be the sum of the two larger numbers and can be eliminated. The estimate of this problem would be about 70, so choices B and C would be too high of a sum.

Do the calculations to confirm.
42.87 + 26.401 = 69.271

21. B
Choice C can be eliminated as it is larger than the starting numbers. 1.602 is about half of 3, so you can eliminate choice D for being too small of a number.

Do the calculations to confirm.
6.363 - 1.602 = 4.761

22. A
Choice C can be eliminated because there are too many numbers after the decimal place.

Do the calculations to confirm.
67.54 – 43.45 = 24.09

23. C
Since 75% can also be written as 75/100, choice D can be eliminated because 75/100 cannot be a whole number. Choices A and B are too small of numbers to be 75/100.

Do the calculations to confirm.

To convert percent to decimal, simply divide the decimal by 100 or move the decimal point 2 places to the left. Therefore, 75 ÷ 100 = 0.75

24. D
Since you can write 39% as 39/100, choice C can be eliminated because a part of 100 will not be a whole number. Choice B is too small of a number to be 39/100.

Do the calculations to confirm.
To convert percent to decimal, simply divide the decimal by 100 or move the decimal point 2 places to the left. Therefore, 39 ÷ 100 = 0.39

25. A
Choice C is close to about 50% of 135, so it can be eliminated. Choice B is 25% of 100, so it can be eliminated as well. Choice D is close to 50 and would be about 33% of 135, leaving you with choice A.

Do the calculations to confirm.
25/100 x 135 = 25 x 1.35 = 33.75

Fraction Tips, Tricks and Shortcuts

When you remember that fractions are just numbers, they become not quite so intimidating. Here are some ideas to keep in mind as you work through fraction math problems:

Remember that a fraction is just a number which names a portion of something. For instance, instead of having a whole pie, a fraction says you have a part of a pie--such as a half of one or a fourth of one.

Two digits make up a fraction. The digit on top is known as the numerator. The digit on the bottom is known as the denominator. To remember which is which, just remember that "denominator" and "down" both start with a "d." And the "downstairs" number is the denominator. So for instance, in ½, the numerator is the 1 and the denominator (or "downstairs") number is the 2.

- It's easy to add two fractions if they have the same denominator. Just add the digits on top and leave the bottom one the same: 1/10 + 6/10 = 7/10.

- It's the same with subtracting fractions with the same denominator: 7/10 - 6/10 = 1/10.

- Adding and subtracting fractions with different denominators is a little more complicated. First, you have to get the problem so that they do have the same denominators. The easiest way to do this is to multiply the denominators For 2/5 + 1/2 multiply 5 by 2. Now you have a denominator of 10. But now you have to change the top numbers too. Since you multiplied the 5 in 2/5 by 2, you also multiply the 2 by 2, to get 4. So the first number is now 4/10. Since you multiplied the second number times 5, you also multiply its top number by 5, to get a final fraction of 5/10. Now you can add 5 and 4 together to get a final sum of 9/10.

- Sometimes you'll be asked to reduce a fraction to its simplest form. This means getting it to where the only common factor of the numerator and denominator is 1. Think of it this way: Numerators and denominators are brothers that must be treated the same. If you do something to one, you must do it to the other, or it's just not fair. For instance, if you divide your numerator by 2, then you should also divide the denominator by the same. Let's take an example: The fraction 2/10 . This is not reduced to its simplest terms because there is a number that will divide evenly into both: the number 2. We want to make it so that the only number that will divide evenly into both is 1. What can we divide into 2 to get 1? The number 2, of course! Now to be "fair," we have to do the same thing to the denominator: Divide 2 into 10 and you get 5. So our new, reduced fraction is 1/5.

- In some ways, multiplying fractions is the easiest of all: Just multiply the two top numbers and then multiply the two bottom numbers. For instance, with this problem: 2/5 X 2/3 you multiply 2 by 2 and get a top number of 4; then multiply 5 by 3 and get a bottom number of 15. Your answer is 4/15.

- Dividing fractions is a bit more involved, but still not too hard. You once again multiply, but only AFTER you have turned the second fraction upside-down. To divide ⅞ by ½, turn the ½ into 2/1, then multiply the top numbers and multiply the bottom numbers: ⅞ X 2/1 gives us 14 on top and 8 on the bottom.

Converting Fractions to Decimals

There are a couple of ways to become good at converting fractions to decimals. One -- the one that will make you the fastest in basic math skills -- is to learn some basic fraction facts. It's a good idea, if you're good at memory, to memorize the following:

1/100 is "one hundredth," expressed as a decimal, it's .01.

1/50 is "two hundredths," expressed as a decimal, it's .02.

1/25 is "one twenty-fifths" or "four hundredths," expressed as a decimal, it's .04.

1/20 is "one twentieth" or ""five hundredths," expressed as a decimal, it's .05.

1/10 is "one tenth," expressed as a decimal, it's .1.

1/8 is "one eighth," or "one hundred twenty-five thousandths," expressed as a decimal, it's .125.

1/5 is "one fifth," or "two tenths," expressed as a decimal, it's .2.

1/4 is "one fourth" or "twenty-five hundredths," expressed as a decimal, it's .25.

1/3 is "one third" or "thirty-three hundredths," expressed as a decimal, it's .33.

1/2 is "one half" or "five tenths," expressed as a decimal, it's .5.

3/4 is "three fourths," or "seventy-five hundredths," expressed as a decimal, it's .75.

Of course, if you're no good at memorization, another good technique for converting a fraction to a decimal is to manipulate it so that the fraction's denominator is 10, 10, 1000, or some other power of 10. Here's an example: We'll start with ¾. What is the first number in the 4 "times table" that you can multiply and get a multiple of 10? Can you multiply 4 by something to get 10? No. Can you multiply it by something to get 100? Yes! 4 X 25 is 100. So let's take that 25 and multiply it by the numerator in our fraction ¾. The numerator is 3, and 3 X 25 is 75. We'll move the decimal in 75 all the way to the left, and we find that ¾ is .75.

We'll do another one: 1/5. Again, we want to find a power of 10 that 5 goes into evenly. Will 5 go into 10? Yes! It goes 2 times. So we'll take that 2 and multiply it by our numerator, 1, and we get 2. We move the decimal in 2 all the way to the left and find that 1/5 is equal to .2.

Converting Fractions to Percent

Working with either fractions or percents can be intimidating enough. But converting from one to the other? That's a genuine nightmare for those who are not math wizards. But really, it doesn't have to be that way. Here are two ways to make it easier to convert a fraction to a percent.

- First, you might remember that a fraction is nothing more than a division problem: you're dividing the bottom number into the top number. So for instance, if we start with a fraction 1/10, we are making a division problem with the 10 on the outside the bracket and the 1 on the inside. As you remember from your lessons on dividing by decimals, since 10 won't go into 1, you add a decimal and make it 10 into 1.0. 10 into 10 goes 1 time, and since it's behind the decimal, it's .1. And how do we say .1? We say "one tenth," which is exactly what we started with: 1/10. So we have a number we can work with now: .1. When we're dealing with percents, though, we're dealing strictly with hundredths (not tenths). You remember from studying decimals that adding a zero to the right of the number on the right side of the decimal does not change the value. Therefore, we can change .1 into .10 and have the same number--except now it's expressed as hundredths. We have 10 hundredths. That's ten out of 100--which is just another way of saying ten percent (ten per hundred or ten out of 100). In other words .1 = .10 = 10 percent. Remember, if you're changing from a decimal to a percent, get rid of the decimal on the left and replace it with a percent mark on the right: 10%. Let's review those steps again: Divide 10 into 1. Since 10 doesn't go into 1, turn 1 into 1.0. Now divide 10 into 1.0. Since 10 goes into 10 1 time, put it there and add your decimal to make it .1. Since a percent is always "hundredths," let's change .1 into .10. Then remove the decimal on the left and replace with a percent sign on the right. The answer is 10%.

- If you are doing these conversions on a multiple-choice test, here's an idea that might be even easier and faster. Let's say you have a fraction of 1/8 and you're asked what the percent is. Since we know that "percent" means hundredths, ask yourself what number we can multiply 8 by to get 100. Since there is no number, ask what number gets us close to 100. That number is 12: 8 X 12 = 96. So it gets us a little less than 100. Now, whatever you do to the denominator, you have to do to the numerator. Let's multiply 1 X 12 and we get 12. However, since 96 is a little less than 100, we know that our answer will be a percent a little MORE than 12%. So if your possible answers on the multiple-choice test are these:

a) 8.5%   b) 19%   c) 12.5%   d) 25%

then we know the answer is c) 12.5%, because it's a little MORE than the 12 we got in our math problem above.

Another way to look at this, using multiple-choice strategy is you know the answer will be "about" 12. Looking at the other choices, they are all too large or too small and can be eliminated right away.

This was an easy example to demonstrate, so don't be fooled! You probably won't get such an easy question on your exam, but the principle holds just the same. By estimating your answer quickly, you can eliminate choices immediately and save precious exam time.

Decimal Tips, Tricks and Shortcuts

Converting Decimals to Fractions
One of the most important tricks for correctly converting a decimal to a fraction doesn't involve math at all. It's simply to learn to say the decimal correctly. If you say "point one" or "point 25" for .1 and .25, you'll have more trouble getting the conversion correct. But if you know that it's called "one tenth" and "twenty-five hundredths," you're on the way to a correct conversion. That's because, if you know your fractions, you know that "one tenth" looks like this: 1/10. And "twenty-five hundredths" looks like this: 25/100.

Even if you have digits before the decimal, such as 3.4, learning how to say the word will help you with the conversion into a fraction. It's not "three point four," it's "three and four tenths." Knowing this, you know that the fraction which looks like "three and four tenths" is 3 4/10.

Of course, your conversion is not complete until you reduce the fraction to its lowest terms: It's not 25/100, but 1/4.

Converting Decimals to Percent

Changing a decimal to a percent is easy if you remember one math formula: multiply by 100. For instance, if you start with .45, you change it to a percent by simply multiplying it by 100. You then wind up with 45. Add the % sign to the end and you get 45%.

That seems easy enough, right? Here think of it this way: You just take out the decimal and stick in a percent sign on the opposite sign. In other words, the decimal on the left is replaced by the % on the right.

It doesn't work quite that easily if the decimal is in the middle of the number. Let's use 3.7 for example. Here, take out the decimal in the middle and replace it with a 0 % at the end. So 3.7 converted to decimal is 370%.

Percent Tips, Tricks and Shortcuts

Percent problems are not nearly as scary as they appear, if you remember this neat trick:

Draw a cross as in:

Portion	Percent
Whole	100

In the upper left, write PORTION. In the bottom left, write WHOLE. In the top right, write PERCENT and in the bottom right, write 100. Whatever your problem is, you will leave blank the unknown, and fill in the other four parts. For example, let's suppose your problem is: Find 10% of 50. Since we know the 10% part, we put 10 in the percent corner. Since the whole number in our problem is 50, we put that in the corner marked whole. You always put 100 underneath the percent, so we leave it as is, which leaves only the top left corner blank. This is where we'll put our answer. Now simply multiply the two corner numbers that are NOT 100. Here, it's 10 X 50. That gives us 500. Now multiply this by the remaining corner, or 100, to get a final answer of 5. 5 is the number that goes in the upper-left corner, and is your final solution. Another hint to remember: Percents are the same thing as hundredths in decimals. So .45 is the same as 45 hundredths or 45 percent.

Converting Percents to Decimals

Percents are simply a specific type of decimals, so it should be no surprise that converting between the two is actually fairly simple. Here are a few tricks and shortcuts to keep in mind:

- Remember that percent means "per 100" or "for every 100." So when you speak of 30% you are saying 30 for every 100 or the fraction 30/100. In basic math, you learned that fractions that have 10 or 100 as the denominator can easily be turned into a decimal. 30/100 is thirty hundredths, or expressed as a decimal, .30.
- Another way to look at it: To convert a percent to a decimal, simply divide the number by 100. So for instance, if the percent is 47%, divide 47 by 100. The result will be .47. Get rid of the % mark and you're done.
- Remember that the easiest way of dividing by 100 is by moving your decimal two spots to the left.

Converting Percents to Fractions

Converting percents to fractions is easy. After all, a percent is nothing except a type of fraction; it tells you what part of 100 that you're talking about. Here are some simple ideas for making the conversion from a percent to a fraction:

- If the percent is a whole number -- say 34% -- then simply write a fraction with 100 as the denominator (the bottom number). Then put the percentage itself on top. So 34% becomes 34/100.
- Now reduce as you would reduce any percent. Here, by dividing 2 into 34 and 2 into 100, you get 17/50.
- If your percent is not a whole number -- say 3.4% --then convert it to a decimal expressed as hundredths. 3.4 is the same as 3.40 (or 3 and forty hundredths). Now ask yourself how you would express "three and forty hundredths" as a fraction. It would, of course, be 3 40/100. Reduce this and it becomes 3 2/5.

Word Problem Multiple-Choice Strategy

Most students find word problems difficult. Tackling Word problems is much easier if you have a systematic approach which we outline below.

Here is the biggest tip for studying Word problems.

Practice regularly and systematically. Sounds simple and easy right? Yes it is, and yes it really does work.

Word problems are a way of thinking and require you to translate a real word problem into mathematical terms.

Some math instructors go so far as to say that learning how to think mathematically is the main reason for teaching word problems.

So what do we mean by Practice regularly and systematically? Studying word problems and math in general requires a logical and mathematical frame of mind. The only way that you can get this is by practicing regularly, which means everyday.

It is critical that you practice word problems everyday for the 5 days before the exam as a bare minimum.

If you practice and miss a day, you have lost the mathematical frame of mind and the benefit of your previous practice is pretty much gone. Anyone who has done any amount of math will agree – you have to practice everyday.

Everything is important. The other critical point about word problems is that all the information given in the problem has some purpose. There is no unnecessary information! Word problems are typically around 50 words in 1 to 3 sentences. If the sometimes complicated relationships are to be explained in that short an explanation, every word has to count. Make sure that you use every piece of information.

Here are 9 simple steps to solving word problems.

Step 1 – Read through the problem at least three times. The first reading should be a quick scan, and the next two readings should be done slowly with a view to finding answers to these important questions:

What does the problem ask? (Usually located towards the end of the problem)

What does the problem imply? (This is usually a point you were asked to remember).

Mark all information, and underline all important words or phrases.

Step 2 – Try to make a pictorial representation of the problem such as a circle and an arrow to show travel. This makes the problem a bit more real and sensible to you.

A favorite word problem is something like, 1 train leaves Station A travelling at 100 km/hr and another train leaves Station B travelling at 60 km/hr. ...

Draw a line, the two stations, and the two trains at either end. This will help solidify the situation in your mind.

Step 3 – Use the information you have to make a table with a blank portion to show information you do not know.

Step 4 – Assign a single letter to represent each unknown data in your table. You can write down the unknown that each letter represents so that you do not make the error of assigning answers to the wrong unknown, because a word problem may have multiple unknowns and you will need to create equations for each unknown.

Step 5 – Translate the English terms in the word problem into a mathematical algebraic equation. Remember that the main problem with word problems is that they are not expressed in regular math equations. You ability to identify correctly the variables and translate the word problem into an equation determines your ability to solve the problem.

Step 6 – Check the equation to see if it looks like regular equations that you are used to seeing and whether it looks sensible. Does the equation appear to represent the information in the question? Take note that you may need to rewrite some formulas needed to solve the word problem equation. For example, word distance problems may need rewriting the distance formula, which is Distance = Time x Rate. If the word problem requires that you solve for time you will need to use Distance/Rate and Distance/Time to solve for Rate. If you understand the distance word problem you should be able to identify the variable you need to solve for.

Step 7 – Use algebra rules to solve the derived equation. Take note that the laws of equation demands that what is done on this side of the equation has to also be done on the other side. You have to solve the equation so that the unknown ends up alone on one side. Where there are multiple unknowns you will need to use elimination or substitution methods to resolve all the equations.

Step 8 – Check your final answers to see if they make sense with the information given in the problem. For example if the word problem involves a discount, the final price should be less or if a product was taxed then the final answer has to cost more.

Step 9 – Cross check your answers by placing the answer or answers in the first equation to replace the unknown or unknowns. If your answer is correct then both side of the equation must equate or equal If your answer is not correct then you may have derived a wrong equation or solved the equation wrongly. Repeat the necessary steps to correct.

Types of Word problems

Word problems can be classified into 12 types. Below are examples of each type with a complete solution. Some types of Word problems can be solved quickly using multiple-choice strategies and some cannot. Always look for ways to estimate the answer and then eliminate choices.

1. Age

A girl is 10 years older than her brother. By next year, she will be twice the age of her brother. What are their ages now?

    a. 25, 15
    b. 19, 9
    c. 21, 11
    d. 29, 19

Solution: B

We will assume that the girl's age is "a" and her brother's is "b." This means that based on the information in the first sentence,
a = 10 +60

Next year, she will be twice her brother's age, which gives
a + 1 = 2(b+1)

We need to solve for one unknown factor and then use the answer to solve for the other. To do this we substitute the value of "a" from the first equation into the second equation. This gives

10+b + 1 = 2b + 2
11 + b = 2b + 2
11 – 2 = 2b – b
b= 9

9 = b this means that her brother is 9 years old.
Solving for the girl's age in the first equation gives

a = 10 + 9
a = 19 the girl is aged 19. So, the girl is aged 19 and the boy is 9

2. Distance or speed

Two boats travel down a river towards the same destination, starting at the same time. One boat is traveling at 52 km/hr, and the other boat at 43 km/hr. How far apart will they be after 40 minutes?

    a. 46.67 km
    b. 19.23 km
    c. 6.03 km
    d. 14.39 km

Solution: C

After 40 minutes, the first boat will have traveled = 52 km/hr x 40 minutes/60 minutes = 34.7 km

After 40 minutes, the second boat will have traveled = 43 km/hr x 40/60 minutes = 28.66 km

Difference between the two boats will be 34.7 km – 28.66 km = 6.03 km

Multiple-Choice Strategy

First estimate the answer. The first boat is travelling 9 km. faster than the second, for 40 minutes, which is 2/3 of an hour. 2/3 of 9 = 6, as a rough guess of the distance apart.

Choices A, B and D can be eliminated right away.

3. Ratio

The instructions in a cookbook states that 700 grams of flour must be mixed in 100 ml of water, and 0.90 grams of salt added. A cook however has just 325 grams of flour. What is the quantity of water and salt that he should use?

    a. 0.41 grams and 46.4 ml
    b. 0.45 grams and 49.3 ml
    c. 0.39 grams and 39.8 ml
    d. 0.25 grams and 40.1 ml

Solution: A

The Cookbook states 700 grams of flour, but the cook only

has 325. The first step is to determine the percentage of flour he has 325/700 x 100 = 46.4%
That means that 46.4% of all other items must also be used.
46.4% of 100 = 46.4 ml of water
46.4% of 0.90 = 0.41 grams of salt.

Multiple-Choice Strategy

The recipe calls for 700 grams of flour but the cook only has 325, which is just less than half, the amount of water and salt are going to be about half.

Choices C and D can be eliminated right away. Choice B is very close so be careful. Looking closely at Choice B, it is exactly half, and since 325 is slightly less than half of 700, it can't be correct.

Choice A is correct.

4. Percent

An agent received $6,685 as his commission for selling a property. If his commission was 13% of the selling price, how much was the property?

    a. $68,825
    b. $121,850
    c. $49,025
    d. $51,423

Solution: D

Let's assume that the property price is x
That means from the information given, 13% of x = 6,685
Solve for x,
x = 6685 x 100/13 = $51,423

Multiple-Choice Strategy

The commission, 13%, is just over 10%, which is easier to work with. Round up $6685 to $6700, and multiple by 10 for an approximate answer. 10 X 6700 = $67,000. You can do this in your head. Choice B is much too big and can be elimi-

nated. Choice C is too small and can be eliminated. Choices A and D are left and good possibilities.
Do the calculations to make the final choice.

5. Sales & Profit

A store owner buys merchandise for $21,045. He transports them for $3,905 and pays his staff $1,450 to stock the merchandise on his shelves. If he does not incur further costs, how much does he need to sell the items to make $5,000 profit?

    a. $32,500
    b. $29,350
    c. $32,400
    d. $31,400

Solution: D

Total cost of the items is $21,045 + $3,905 + $1,450 = $26,400
Total cost is now $26,400 + $5000 profit = $31,400

Multiple-Choice Strategy

Round off and add the numbers up in your head quickly. 21,000 + 4,000 + 1500 = 26500. Add in 5000 profit for a total of 31500.

Choice B is too small and can be eliminated. Choice C and Choice A are too large and can be eliminated.

6. Tax/Income

A woman earns $42,000 per month and pays 5% tax on her monthly income. If the Government increases her monthly taxes by $1,500, what is her income after tax?

    a. $38,400
    b. $36,050
    c. $40,500
    d. $39, 500

Solution: A

Initial tax on income was 5/100 x 42,000 = $2,100
$1,500 was added to the tax to give $2,100 + 1,500 = $3,600
Income after tax left is $42,000 - $3,600 = $38,400

7. Interest

A man invests $3000 in a 2-year term deposit that pays 3% interest per year. How much will he have at the end of the 2-year term?

    a. $5,200
    b. $3,020
    c. $3,182.7
    d. $3,000

Solution: C

This is a compound interest problem. The funds are invested for 2 years and interest is paid yearly, so in the second year, he will earn interest on the interest paid in the first year.

3% interest in the first year = 3/100 x 3,000 = $90
At end of first year, total amount = 3,000 + 90 = $3,090
Second year = 3/100 x 3,090 = 92.7.
At end of second year, total amount = $3090 + $92.7 = $3,182.7

8. Averaging

The average weight of 10 books is 54 grams. 2 more books were added and the average weight became 55.4. If one of the 2 new books added weighed 62.8 g, what is the weight of the other?

    a. 44.7 g
    b. 67.4 g
    c. 62 g
    d. 52 g

Solution: C

Total weight of 10 books with average 54 grams will be = 10×54 = 540 g
Total weight of 12 books with average 55.4 will be = 55.4×12 = 664.8 g
So total weight of the remaining 2 will be = 664.8 − 540 = 124.8 g
If one weighs 62.8, the weight of the other will be = 124.8 g − 62.8 g = 62 g

Multiple-Choice Strategy

Averaging problems can be estimated by looking at which direction the average goes. If additional items are added and the average goes up, the new items much be greater than the average. If the average goes down after new items are added, the new items must be less than the average.

Here, the average is 54 grams and 2 books are added which increases the average to 55.4, so the new books must weight more than 54 grams.

Choices A and D can be eliminated right away.

9. Probability

A bag contains 15 marbles of various colors. If 3 marbles are white, 5 are red and the rest are black, what is the probability of randomly picking out a black marble from the bag?

    a. 7/15
    b. 3/15
    c. 1/5
    d. 4/15

Solution: A

Total marbles = 15
Number of black marbles = 15 − (3 + 5) = 7
Probability of picking out a black marble = 7/15

10. Two Variables

A company paid a total of $2850 to book for 6 single rooms and 4 double rooms in a hotel for one night. Another company paid $3185 to book for 13 single rooms for one night in the same hotel. What is the cost for single and double rooms in that hotel?

    a. single= $250 and double = $345
    b. single= $254 and double = $350
    c. single = $245 and double = $305
    d. single = $245 and double = $345

Solution: D

We can determine the price of single rooms from the information given of the second company. 13 single rooms = 3185.
One single room = 3185 / 13 = 245
The first company paid for 6 single rooms at $245. 245 x 6 = $1470
Total amount paid for 4 double rooms by first company = $2850 - $1470 = $1380
Cost per double room = 1380 / 4 = $345

11. Geometry

The length of a rectangle is 5 in. more than its width. The perimeter of the rectangle is 26 in. What is the width and length of the rectangle?

    a. width = 6 inches, Length = 9 inches
    b. width = 4 inches, Length = 9 inches
    c. width =4 inches, Length = 5 inches
    d. width = 6 inches, Length = 11 inches

Solution: B

Formula for perimeter of a rectangle is 2(L + W)
p=26, so 2(L+W) = p
The length is 5 inches more than the width, so
2(w+5) + 2w = 26
2w + 10 + 2w = 26

2w + 2w = 26 - 10
4w = 16

W = 16/4 = 4 inches

L is 5 inches more than w, so L = 5 + 4 = 9 inches.

12. Totals and fractions

A basket contains 125 oranges, mangos and apples. If 3/5 of the fruits in the basket are mangos and only 2/5 of the mangos are ripe, how many ripe mangos are there in the basket?

    a. 30
    b. 68
    c. 55
    d. 47

Solution: A
Number of mangos in the basket is 3/5 x 125 = 75
Number of ripe mangos = 2/5 x 75 = 30

Answer Sheet

1. (A) (B) (C) (D)
2. (A) (B) (C) (D)
3. (A) (B) (C) (D)
4. (A) (B) (C) (D)
5. (A) (B) (C) (D)
6. (A) (B) (C) (D)
7. (A) (B) (C) (D)
8. (A) (B) (C) (D)
9. (A) (B) (C) (D)
10. (A) (B) (C) (D)

Practice Questions

1. The average weight of 13 students in a class of 15 (two were absent that day) is 42 kg. When the remaining two are weighed, the average became 42.7 kg. If one of the remaining students weighs 48 kg., how much does the other weigh?

    a. 44.7 kg.
    b. 45.6 kg.
    c. 46.5 kg.
    d. 41.4 kg.

2. Brad has agreed to buy everyone a Coke. Each drink costs $1.89, and there are 5 friends. Estimate Brad's cost.

    a. $7
    b. $8
    c. $10
    d. $12

3. At the beginning of 2009, Madalyn invested $5,000 in a savings account. The account pays 4% interest per year. How much will Madalyn have in the account in 2 years?

    a. $5,408
    b. $5,200
    c. $5,110
    d. $7,000

4. The cost of waterproofing canvas is .50 a square yard. What's the total cost for waterproofing a canvas truck cover that is 15' x 24'?

    a. $18.00
    b. $6.67
    c. $180.00
    d. $20.00

5. John is a barber and receives 40% of the amount paid by each of his customers, and all of any tips paid to him. If a man pays $8.50 for a haircut and tips $1.30, how much money does John receive?

    a. $3.92
    b. $4.70
    c. $5.70
    d. $6.40

6. Two trains start their journey at the same time, one with average speed of 72 km/hr and other with 52 km/hr. How far apart are the trains after 20 minutes?

    a. 6.67 km
    b. 17.33 km
    c. 24.3 km
    d. 41.33 km

7. John purchased a jacket at a 7% discount. He had a membership and received an additional discount of 1.6%. If he paid $425, what is the retail price of the jacket?

    a. $448
    b. $460
    c. $466
    d. $472

8. A store sells stereos for $545. If 15% of the cost was added to the price as value added tax, what is the total cost?

   a. $490.4
   b. $626.75
   c. $575.00
   d. $590.15

9. A car covers a certain distance in 3.5 hours at an average speed of 60 km/hr. How much time in hours will a motorbike take to cover the same distance at an average speed of 40 km/hr?

   a. 4.5
   b. 4.75
   c. 5.25
   d. 5

10. Jim left home for the office at 7:00 am. He reached his office at 7:48 am. How far is his house from office if his average driving speed is 40km/hr?

    a. 32 km
    b. 34 km
    c. 38 km
    d. 40 km

Answer Key

1. C
Total weight of 13 students with average 42 will be = 42 × 13 = 546 kg.
Total weight of 15 students with average 42.7 will be = 42.7 × 15 = 640.5 kg. So total weight of the remaining 2 will be = 640.5 - 546 = 94.5 kg. Weight of the other will be = 94.5 – 48 = 46.5 kg

Multiple-Choice Strategy

When the 2 additional students were added, the average went up, so the they must weigh more than the average. Choice D is less than the average so it can be eliminated right away.

2. C
If there are 5 friends and each drink costs $1.89, we can round up to $2 per drink and estimate the total cost at, 5 X $2 = $10.

The actual, cost is 5 X $1.89 = $9.45.

3. A
This is a compound interest problem. Interest is paid out at the end of the first year and added to the account, and then interest is paid on the new total in the second year.

First do a quick calculation in your head, using numbers that are easy to work with. 5000 X 10% = 500 and so 5% will be half of that which is $250. If we ignore the compounding (interest on interest) in the second year, we have an approximate total of $5500, which is a high approximation.

Choice D can be eliminated as much too high, and choice C is too low. Choice B is about the total for one years interest so it can also be eliminated. Choice A is the only choice left.

Do the calculations to confirm.

5000 X 4% = 200
In the second year, 5200 X 4% = 208

So the total at the end of the second year is $5,408.

4. D
This is a square foot cost problem. The problem is to find the total square footage, and the multiply by the cost.

Use math shortcuts to calculate the answer in your head. First calculate total square feet, which is $15 \cdot 24 = 360$ ft². Next, convert this value to square yards, (1 yards² = 9 ft²) which is $360/9 = 40$ yards². At $0.50 per square yard, the total cost is $40 \cdot 0.50$ (or half) = $20.

This is actually the correct answer choice D.

5. B
Estimate the answer in your head quickly. 40% is close to 50%, which is half. 50% of $8.50 is 4.25 plus tips of $1.30 is 5.55 approximately.

Looking at the options, choices A and D can all be eliminated as too low or too high, leaving choice B and C. C is probably too high, as 5.55 is an approximation and so choice B is looking correct.

Do the calculations to confirm.
8.5 X 40/100 = 3.40 + 1.30 = $4.70.

6. A
First estimate the answer quickly in your head. One train is travelling at 72 km. and the other at 52 km. In one hour they will be 20 km. apart, so in 20 minutes they will be 20/3 = about 6.5 km.

Looking at the options, choices B and C are far to big and can be eliminated. Choice D is closer, but still too large, and can also be eliminated.

Do the calculations to confirm.
Distance traveled by 1st train in 20 minute = (72 km/hr×20 minutes)/60 minutes=24 km
Distance traveled by 2nd train in 20 minute = (52 km/hr×20 minutes)/60 minutes=17.33 km
Difference in distance=24-17.33=6.67 km

7. C
Make a rough estimate in your head. Use 10% instead of 7%, so 425 + 10% = 467. Ignore the 1.6% for now and remember this is an estimate on the high side.

Choice A is too small and can be eliminated and choice D is too high and can be eliminated. That leaves choices B and C.

Do the calculations to confirm.
Let the original price be x, then at rate of 7% the discounted price will be=0.93x
2% discounted amount then will be = 0.02 × 0.93x = 0.0186x
Remaining price = 0.93x - 0.0186x = 0.9114x
This is the amount which John has paid so
0.9114x = 425
x = 425/ 0.9114
x = $466.31

8. B
This question can be estimated in your head with a few shortcuts. 15% is difficult to work with so use 10% and 5%.
10% of 545 = 54.5
5% of 545 = about 27 (half of 10%)
Add them quickly in your head by estimating again. Take 50 + 25 = 75 and add 7 for a rough approximation of 82. The actual number is 81.5.
Add 82 to 545. Again round to easy numbers to work with. take 550 + 82 = 632. Remember this is a high estimate. (The actual figure is 626.5)

Looking at the options, the only choice over 600 is Choice B.

Confirm by doing the calculations.
Actual cost = X, therefore, X = 545 + (545 X 0.15)
X = 545 + 81.75
X = 626.75

9. C
Estimate the answer first. The car is travelling at 60 km. and the motorbike is travelling at 40 km., which is 2/3 (40/60 = 2/3, or 2:3). So the motorcycle will take one-third longer to travel the same distance. If the car took 3.5 hours, the motorbike will take 3.5 + (1/3 of 3.5). 1/3 of 3.5 is going to be about 1.1, or say 1. 3.5 + 1 = 4.5.

Looking at the options, choice D can be eliminated right away. Choice A can be eliminated since it equals our estimate.

Do the calculations to confirm.
The distance covered by the car = 60 X 3.5 = 210 km.
Time required by the motorbike = 210/40 = 5.25 hr.

10. A
Do a quick estimate in your head and see if any options can be eliminated. Jim is travelling for 48 minutes at 40 km. per hour. If he was travelling for one hour, he would cover 40 km. Right away choice D can be eliminated because he is only travelling for a portion of an hour. Choice C, 38 km. is a very unlikely choice because it is so close to 40 and can be eliminated. The answer will be choice A or B.

Do the calculations to confirm.
Time to reach the office = 48 minutes. So if he covers 40 km in 60 minutes, then in 48 minutes, he will cover 48 X 40/60 = 32 km.

How to Write an Essay

Writing an essay can be a difficult process, especially if you are under time constraints such as during an exam. Here are three simple steps to help you to write a solid, well thought out essay:

1. **Brainstorm** potential themes and general ideas for your essay.
2. **Outline** your essay step by step, including subheadings for ease of understanding.
3. **Write** your essay carefully being aware of proper grammar and sentence structure.

Brainstorming

You should first spend time thinking about the general subject of the essay. If the essay is asking a question, you must make sure to answer this fully in your essay. You may find it helpful to highlight key words in your assignment or use a simple spider diagram to jot down key ideas.

Example

Read the following information and complete the following assignment:

Joseph Conrad is a Polish author who lived in England for most of his life and wrote a prolific amount of English literature. Much of his work was completed during the height of the British Empire's colonial imperialism.

Assignment: What impact has Joseph Conrad had on modern society? Present your point of view on the matter and support it with evidence. Your evidence may include reasoning, logic, examples from readings, your own experience, and observations.

Joseph Conrad

> **Background?** sailor, adventure, Polish immigrant, Youth, Nostromo, Heart of Darkness
> **Themes in his works?** ivory, silver trading, colonialism, corruption, greed
> **Thoughts?** descent into madness, nature of evil

Outlining (or planning)

An outline or plan is critical to organize your thoughts and ideas fully and logically. There are many ways to do this; the easiest is to write down the following headings:

1. Title
2. Introduction
3. Body
4. Conclusion

You should then jot down key ideas and themes that fit logically under the appropriate heading. This plan is now the backbone of your essay.

Tip: Even if you are not required to produce an outline or plan for the assignment, you should always leave it with your essay in the exam booklet or the back of the assignment paper. Simply draw a line across it and write 'plan' or 'outline'. This demonstrates to the reader the approach you use in formulating and finally writing your essay.

Writing the essay

Your introduction is what will help the reader to decide whether they want to read the rest of your essay. The introduction also introduces the subject matter and allows you to provide a general background to the reader. The first sentence is very important and you should avoid starting the essay with openers such as 'I will be comparing...'

Example

> Born as Józef Teodor Konrad Korzeniowski on December 3rd, 1857, Joseph Conrad led

an adventurous life. As a Polish immigrant, Conrad never quite fit into England where he spent most of his adult life. As a younger man, Conrad made a living off sailing voyages. These swashbuckling experiences soon had him writing tales of the high seas such as one of his first works, Youth. While his early, adventurous work was of high quality, Conrad is best remembered for shedding light on the exploitative side of colonialism. Age and experience led him to start writing about (and challenging) the darker side of the imperial way of thinking. Conrad's work has forever soured words such as colonialism and imperialism.

In the main part, or body of your essay, you should always be yourself and be original.

- Avoid using clichés.
- Be aware of your tone.
- Consider the language that you use. Avoid jargon and slang. Use clear prose and imagery.
- Your writing should always flow; remember to use transitions, especially between paragraphs. Read aloud in your head to make sure a paragraph sounds right.
- Always try to use a new paragraph for new ideas.

Example

Conrad's written fiction focused on themes such as greed and power. He portrayed these two concepts as purveyors of evil. Greed and power may take on different guises, but the end result would always be the same.

Perhaps his most famous piece, The Heart of Darkness, is about the descent of an English ivory trader, Mr. Kurtz, into madness. We are taken up a river resembling the Congo by a narrator, Marlow, who is sent to retrieve Mr. Kurtz. Marlow eventually finds that Kurtz has been diluted by power and greed, the two things that spurred on colonialism in Africa. Kurtz has

> taken charge of a large tribe of natives (that
> he brutalizes) and has been hoarding ivory for
> himself.
>
> Much of Conrad's later work was cut from
> the same vein as The Heart of Darkness. His
> crowning achievement is considered Nostromo
> where he takes an idealistic hero and corrupts
> him with colonial greed. Only this time the greed
> is for silver, not ivory.
>
> Conrad's work resonates with readers partly
> because it was semi-autobiographical. Where
> his experience sailing the high seas helped
> bring his adventure stories to light, likewise did
> his experience witnessing atrocities in Africa
> reverberate through his writing.

The conclusion is your last chance to impress your reader and brings your entire essay to a logical close. You may want to link your conclusion back to your introduction or provide some closing statements. Do not panic if you cannot close your essay off completely. Few subjects offer closure.

Your conclusion should always be consistent with the rest of the essay and you should never introduce a new idea in your conclusion. It is also important to remember that a weak conclusion can diminish the impact of a good essay.

Example

> In sum, Joseph Conrad's life experiences and
> masterful writing left a lasting impact on the
> image of progress and what it meant to "move
> forward." He brought to light the cost in human
> lives that was required for Europe to continue
> mining natural resources from foreign lands.
> Joseph Conrad had a permanent impact on
> imperial culture, and colonial brutality has
> been on the decline ever since his work was
> published.

Presentation

Poor grammar and punctuation can ruin an otherwise good essay. You should always follow any requirements about the presentation of your essay, such as word count. You should also make sure that your writing is legible. Always allow time for one final read-through before submission.

Tip: If you are able to, write with double spacing. If you make a mistake, you can cross it out and write the correction on the blank line above.

Some final points to think about for writing a solid, well thought out essay:

- A good essay will contain a strong focus.
- There is no set essay structure but you can use subheadings for better readability.
- Avoid particularly sensitive or controversial material. If you must write about something controversial, always make sure to include counter arguments.
- Your essay may have little to do with the subject itself; it is about what you make of the subject.
- Your essay can include examples from your readings, experience, studies or observations.
- Spend time doing practice essays and looking at sample essays beforehand.

Another Example

Lets look at another example using the three steps required to write a good essay:

1. **Brainstorming**
2. **Outlining**
3. **Writing**

Using a second essay, we can now explore these three steps in further detail.

Brainstorming
Example

> *Think about the information that follows and the assignment below.*
>
> *People often quote the last two lines of Robert Frost's "The Road not Taken" as being metaphorical for success. The line's read "I took the one less travelled by, / And that has made all the difference" (19, 20).*
>
> *Assignment: Analyze and interpret this poem. Consider the poem's place in Modernist culture and Robert Frost's personal experiences. Read in between the lines and identify the more complex aspects/themes of this poem. Outline and complete an essay that challenges the point of view presented above, that the poem is synonymous with success. Provide evidence backed up by logic, experience, research, and/or examples from the poem.*

The assignment and key words that appear in the brief above are being highlighted. This confirms that the essay is not asking a specific question, but it is asking for discussion of the subject matter and phrases
This is the time to take a few moments to jot down initial thoughts about the assignment. Do not worry too much about proper grammar at this point, just get all your thoughts down on paper:

"The Road Not Taken" by Robert Frost

> **Background?** Modernist poetry
> **Themes?** Life decisions, regret, fate, the unknown future
> **Thoughts?** The diverging roads are symbolic, the sigh at end signifies regret, life has many twists and turns, you can end in a drastically different situation later after a simple decision now

Outlining (or Planning)

Outlining or planning is the next important stage in the process and you should always spend a few minutes writing a plan. This plan is just as important as the essay itself. You can also note how much **time** you may want to spend on a particular section. Make sure to assign headings to each main section of the essay and include important questions/themes you want to address.

Example

> **1. Title**
>
> **2. Essay introduction**
> *Identify and discuss the underlying theme/s in Robert Frost's "The Road Not Taken"*
> *What was Frost's background and its applicability to understanding this poem?*
>
> **3. Essay body**
> *Quick summary of the poem*
> *Discuss key themes and other concepts*
> *Discuss how these things relate to Modernism*
>
> **4. Essay conclusion**
> *Rephrase the themes of Robert Frost's poem and their place in modernist doctrine*

This plan is now the outline for the essay.

Writing the Essay

The introduction is important, as it needs to introduce the reader to the essay in a way that will encourage them to continue reading. A good introduction will introduce the subject matter to a reader and point out relevant information that may be helpful to know when reading the rest of the essay.

Example

> Identify and discuss the underlying theme/s in

Robert Frost's "The Road Not Taken"

Robert Frost wrote during the artistic movement after World War I known as Modernism. One purpose of modernism was to remake things in a new light, to analyze and change symptoms of societies that had plunged the European world into a grisly war. Frost's poem, "The Road Not Taken," carries with it a burden of regret that was a staple of Modernist art.

This introduction opens with what explaining about the time period of Robert Frost and real life influences to the theme of his poem, "The Road Not Taken." It contains some powerful language that will encourage the reader to continue reading and gives a solid base in understanding the remainder of the essay.

The main part or **body of the essay** is also very important:

Example

"The Road Not Taken" was almost assuredly influenced by Robert Frost's personal life. He was very familiar with facing difficult decisions. Frost had to make the decision to send both his sister and daughter to mental institutions. His son Carol committed suicide at the age of 38. The list of loss Frost experienced in his life goes on, but it suffices to say he was familiar with questioning the past.

With no other hints of the narrator's identity, it is best to assume that he is a man similar to Frost himself. The poem itself is about a nameless narrator reflecting on when he travelled through the autumn woods one day. He had come across a split in the road and expresses regret that he could not travel both. Each road is described as looking similar and as having equal wear but it is also mentioned one was grassier. The roads were unknown to the narrator, and shared equal possibilities in how well they may or may not be around their bends.   He tells his listener with a sigh that he had made his decision and had taken

> "the road less travelled by" (19). Even though he had little idea which road would be better in the long run, the one he chose proved difficult.
>
> This poem is a collection of all the insecurities and possibilities that come with even the simplest decisions. We experience the sorrow expressed by the narrator in the opening lines with every decision we make. For all the choices you make in life, there is a counterweight of choices you have not made. In a way, we are all missing half of our lives' possibilities. This realization causes a mixture of regret and nostalgia, but also stokes in us the keen awareness these missed opportunities are inevitable and regretting them is a waste of energy. We often find ourselves stuck, as the narrator is, between questioning the decisions we've made and knowing that this natural process isn't exactly productive.
>
> Unsolvable regret and nostalgia are things that the Modernists fought with on a regular basis. They often experimented in taking happenings of the past and reinventing them to fit a new future.

The body of the essay opens with providing a brief overview of Robert Frost's personal life and his life's relevance to the over arching theme of dealing with difficult decisions in the poem, "The Road Not Taken."

A new paragraph starts where appropriate and at the end of the discussion of Robert Frost's life, a **transition** moves the reader back to the start of the book (closing off this section). This helps to move the reader towards the next discussion point.

The tone of this essay is formal, mainly because of the seriousness of the subject – regret and nostalgia plays a major role in people's lives all around the world.

For the conclusion, there will be a summary of the main discussion. While it is ideal for you to impress the reader with your writing, more importantly, you need to make sure you cover all your bases and address the assignment appropriately with a closing statement about any important points you discussed in the body of your essay.

Example

> In conclusion, Robert Frost's poem "The Road Not Taken" deals with themes of fate, regret, sorrow, and the many possibilities our decisions hold. Consider how easy it would be to upturn your life today if you made a few decisions you normally wouldn't. Frost's poem forces us to consider the twists and turns our lives take. Perhaps with a sigh, we could all think about the choices that for us have made all the difference.

This conclusion is consistent with the rest of the essay in terms of style. There are no new ideas introduced and it has referred to the main points in the assignment title.

Finally, a full read-through is necessary before submission. It only takes a couple of minutes to read through and pick up any errors. Remember to double space to leave room for any corrections to be made. You can also leave spacing at the end of each paragraph if you should need to add an additional sentence or two.

Common Essay Mistakes - Example 1

Whether the topic is love or action, reality television shows damage society. Viewers witness the personal struggles of strangers and they experience an outpouring of emotions in the name of entertainment. This can be dangerous on many levels. Viewers become numb to real emotions and values. Run the risk of not interpreting a dangerous situation correctly. 1 The reality show participant is also at risk because they are completely exposed. 2 The damage to both viewers and participants leads to the destruction of our healthy societal values.

Romance reality shows are dangerous to the participants and contribute to the emotional problems witnessed in society today as we set up a system built on equality and respect, shows like "The Bachelor" tear it down. 3 In front of millions of viewers every week, young women compete for a man. Twenty-five women claim to be in love with a man they just met. The man is reduced to an object they compete for. There are tears, fights, and manipulation aimed at winning the prize. 4 Imagine a young woman's reality when she returns home and faces the scrutiny of viewers who watched her unravel on television every Monday night. These women objectify themselves and have learned 5 that relationships are a combination of hysteria and competition. This does not give hope to a society based on family values and equality.

6 While incorporating the same manipulations and breakdown of relationships offered on "The Bachelor," shows like "Survivor" add another level of danger. Not only are they building a society based on lying to each other, they are competing in physical challenges that become dangerous. In the name of entertainment, these challenges become increasingly physical and are usually held in a hostile environment. The viewer's ability to determine the safety of an activity is messed up. 7 To entertain and preserve their pride, participants continue in competitions regardless of the danger level. For example, 8 participants on "Survivor" have sustained serious injuries in the form of heart attack and burns. Societal rules are based on the safety of its citizens, not on hurting yourself for entertainment.

    Reality shows of all kinds are dangerous to participants. They damage society. 9

1. Correct sentence fragments. Who/what runs the risk? Add a subject or combine sentences. Try: "Viewers become numb to real emotions and run the risk of not interpreting a dangerous situation correctly."

2. Correct redundant phrases. Try: "The reality show participant is also at risk because they are exposed."

3. Correct run-on sentences. Decide which thoughts should be separated. Try: "Romance reality shows are dangerous to participants and contribute to the emotional problems of society today. As we support a system built on equality and respect, shows like "The Bachelor" tear it down."

4. Vary sentence structure and length. Try: "Twenty-five women claim to be in love with a man who is reduced to being the object of competition. There are tears, fights, and manipulation aimed at winning the prize."

5. Use active voice. Try: These women objectify themselves and learned that relationships are a combination of hysteria and competition.

6. Use transitions to tie paragraphs together. Try: Start the paragraph with, "Action oriented reality shows are equally as dangerous to the participants."

7. Avoid casual language/slang. Try: "The viewer's ability to determine the safety of an activity is compromised."

8. Don't address the essay. Avoid phrases like "for example" and "in conclusion." Try: "Participants on "Survivor" have sustained serious injuries as heart attack and burns.

9. Leave yourself time to write a strong conclusion! Try: Designate 3-5 minutes for writing your conclusion.

Common Essay Mistakes - Example 2

Questioning authority makes society stronger. In every aspect our society, there is an authoritative person or group making rules. There is also the group underneath them who are meant to follow. 1 This is true of our country's public schools as well as our federal government. The right to question authority at both of these levels is guaranteed by the United States Declaration of Independence. People are given the ability to question so that authority figures are kept in check 2 and will be forced to listen to the opinions of other people. Questioning authority leads to positive changes in society and preserves what is already working well.

If students never question the authority of a principal's decisions, the best interest of the student body is lost. Good things 3 may not remain in place for the students and no amendment to the rules are sought. Change requires that authority be questioned. An example of this is Silver Head Middle School in Davie, Florida. Last year, the principal felt strongly about enforcing the school's uniform policy. Some students were not bothered by this. 4 Many students felt the policy disregarded their civil rights. A petition voicing student dissatisfaction was signed and presented to the principal. He met with a student representative to discuss the petition. Compromise was reached as a monthly "casual day." The students were able to promote change and peace by questioning authority.

Even at the level of federal government, our country's ultimate authority, the ability to question is the key to the harmony keeping society strong. Most government officials are elected by the public so they have the right to question their authority. 5 If there's a mandate, law, or statement that citizens aren't 6 happy with, they have recourse. Campaigning for or against a political platform and participating in the electoral process give a voice to every opinion. I think elections are very important. 7 Without this questioning and examination of society's laws, the government will represent only the voice of the authority figure. The success of our society is based on the questioning of authority. 8

Society is strengthened by those who question authority. Dialogue is created between people with different visions and change becomes possible. At both the level of public school and of federal government, the positive effects of questioning authority can be witnessed. Whether questioning the decisions of a single principal or the motives of the federal government, it is the willingness of people to question and create change that allows society to grow. A strong society is inspired by many voices, all at different levels. 9 These voices keep society strong.

1. **Write concisely.** Combine the sentences to improve understanding and cut unnecessary words. Try: "In every aspect of society, there is an authority making rules and a group of people meant to follow them."

2. **Avoid slang.** Re-word "kept in check." Try: "People are given the ability to question so that authority figures are held

accountable and will be forced to listen to the opinions of other people.

2-2. Cut unnecessary words. Try: "People are given the ability to question so that authority figures are held accountable and will listen to other opinions."

3. Use precise language. What are "good things?" Try: "Interesting activities may not remain in place for the students and no amendment to the rules are sought."

Use correct subject-verb agreement. Be careful to identify the correct subject of your sentence. Try: "Interesting activities may not remain in place for the students and no amendment to the rules is sought."

4. Don't add information that doesn't add value to your argument. Cut: "Some students weren't bothered by this."

5. Check for parallel structure. Who has the right to question whose authority? Try: "Having voted them in, the people have the authority to question public officials."

6. Don't use contractions in academic essays. Try: "If there is a mandate, law, or statement that citizens are not happy with, they have recourse."

7. Don't use the pronoun "I" in persuasive essays. Cut opinions. Cut: "I think elections are very important."

8. Use specific examples to prove your argument. Try: Discuss a particular election in depth.

9. Cut redundant sentences. Cut: "A strong society is inspired by many voices, all at different levels."

Writing Concisely

Concise writing is direct and descriptive. The reader follows the writer's thoughts easily. If your writing is concise, a four paragraph essay is acceptable for standardized tests. It's better to write clearly about fewer ideas than to write poorly about many.

This doesn't always mean using fewer words. It means that every word you use is important to the message. Unnecessary or repetitive information dilutes ideas and weakens your writing. The meaning of the word concise comes from the Latin, "to cut up." If it isn't necessary information, don't waste precious testing minutes writing it down.

Being redundant is a quick way to lengthen a sentence or paragraph, but it takes away your power during a timed essay. While many writers use repetition of phrases and key words to make their point, it's important to remove words that don't add value. Redundancy can confuse and lead you away from your subject when you need to write quickly. Be aware that many redundant phrases are part of our daily language and need to be cut from your essay.

For example, "bouquet of flowers" is a redundant phrase as only the word "bouquet" is necessary. Its definition includes flowers. Be especially careful with words you use to stress a point, such as "completely," "totally," and "very."

First of all, I'd like to thank my family.
Revised: First, I'd like to thank my family.

The school *introduced a new* rule.
Revised: The school introduced a rule.

I am *completely full*.
Revised: I am full.

Your glass is *totally empty*!
Revised: Your glass is empty!

Her artwork is *very unique*.
Revised: Her artwork is unique.

Other ways to cut bulk and time include avoiding phrases that have no meaning or power in your essay. Phrases like "in my opinion," "as a matter of fact," and "due to the fact that" are space and time wasters. Also, change passive verbs to active voice.

In my opinion, the paper is well written.
Revised: The paper is well written.

The book *was written* by the best students.
Revised: The best students wrote the book.

The teacher *is listening* to the students.
The teacher listens to the students.

This assigns action to the subject, shortens, and clarifies the sentence. When time is working against you, precise language is on your side.

Not only should you remove redundant phrases, whole sentences without value should be cut too. Replacing general nouns with specific ones is an effective way to accomplish this.

She screamed as the thing came closer. It was a sharp-toothed dog.
Revised: She screamed as the sharp-toothed dog came closer.

The revised sentence is precise and the paragraph is improved by combining sentences and varying sentence structure. When editing, ask yourself which thoughts should be connected and which need to be separated. Skim each paragraph as you finish writing it and cut as you go.

Leave three to four minutes for final editing. While reading, make a point to pause at every period. This allows you to "hear" sentences the way your reader will, not how you meant them to sound. This will help you find the phrases and sentences that need to be cut or combined. The result is an essay a grader will appreciate.

Avoiding Redundancy

Duplication and verbosity in English is the use of two or more words that clearly mean the same thing, making one of them unnecessary. It is easy to do use redundant expressions or phrases in a conversation where speech is spontaneous, and common in spoken English. In written English, however, redundancy is more serious and harder to ignore. Here is a list of redundant phrases to avoid.

1. Suddenly exploded.

An explosion is instantaneous or immediate and that is sudden enough. No need to use 'suddenly' along with exploded.

2. Final outcome.

An outcome refers to the result. An outcome is intrinsically final and so no need to use final along with outcome.

3. Advance notice/planning/reservations/ warning.

A warning, notice, reservation or plan is made before an event. Once the reader sees any of these words, they know that they were done or carried out before the event. These words do not need to be used with advance.

4. First began, new beginning.

Beginning signals the start or the first time, and therefore the use of "new" is superfluous.

5. Add an additional.

The word 'add' indicates the provision of another something, and so "additional" is superfluous.

6. For a period/number of days.

The word "days" is already in plural and clearly signifies more than just one day. It is thus redundant to use "a number of," or "a period of" along with days. Simply state the number of days or of the specific number of days is unknown, you say 'many days.'

7. Foreign imports.

Imports are foreign as they come from another country, so it is superfluous to refer to imports as "foreign."

8. Forever and ever.

Forever indicates eternity and so there is no need for "ever" as it simply duplicated forever.

9. Came at a time when.

"At a time" is not necessary in this phrase because the 'when' already provides a temporal reference to the action, coming.

10. Free gift.

It cannot be a gift if it is paid for. A gift, by nature, is free and so referring to a gift is free is redundant.

11. Collaborate/join/meet/merge together.

The words merge, join, meet and collaborate already suggest people or things coming together. It is unnecessary to use any of these words with together, such as saying merge together or join together. The correct expression is to simply say join or merge, omitting the together.

12. Invited guests.

Guests are those invited for an event. Since they had to be invited to be guests, there is no need to use invited with guests.

13. Major breakthrough.

A breakthrough is significant by nature. It can only be described as a breakthrough when there is a notable progress. The significant nature of the progress is already implied when you use the word "breakthrough," so "major" is redundant.

14. Absolutely certain or sure/essential/ guaranteed.

When someone or something is said to be sure or certain it indicates that it is without doubt. Using "absolutely" in addition to certain, or sure is unnecessary. Essential or guaranteed is used for something that is absolute and so also does not need the word absolutely to accompany them.

15. Ask a question.

Ask means to present a question. Using "question" in addition to "ask" is redundant.

16. Basic fundamentals/essentials.

Using basic here is redundant. Essentials and fundamental suggest an elementary nature.

17. [Number] a.m. in the morning/p.m. in the evening.

When you write 8 a.m. the reader knows you mean 8 o'clock in the morning. It is not necessary to say 8 a.m. in the morning. Simply write 8 a.m. or 8 p.m.

18. Definite decision.

A decision is already definite even if it can be reversed later. A decision is a definite course of action has been chosen. No need to use the word definite along with the word decision.

19. Past history/record.

A record or history by definition refers to past events or occurrences. Using past to qualify history or record is unnecessary.

20. Consensus of opinion.

Consensus means agreement over something that may be or not be an opinion. So it may look that using the phrase 'consensus of opinion' is appropriate, but it is better to omit "opinion."

21. Enter in.

Enter means going in, as no one enters out. Therefore no need to add "in," simply use "enter."

22. Plan ahead.

You cannot plan for the past. Planning can only be done for

the future. When you use "plan," the future is already implied.

23. Possibly might.

The words might and possibly signify probability, so just use one at a time.

24. Direct confrontation.

A confrontation is a head-on conflict, and does not need to be modified with "direct."

25. Postpone until later.

Something postponed is delayed or moved to a later time, and does not need to be modified with "later."

26. False pretense.

The word pretense is only used to describe a deception, so a "false" pretense is redundant.

27. Protest against.

Protest involves showing opposition; there is no need to use against.

28. End result.

Result only comes at the end. The reader who sees the word 'result' already knows that it occurs at the end.

29. Estimated at about/roughly.

Estimates are approximations that are not expected to be accurate, and do not need to be modified with "roughly" or "about."

30. Repeat again.

Repeat refers to something done again and does not need to be modified with "again."

31. Difficult dilemma.

A dilemma is a situation that is complicated or difficult, and does not need to be modified with "difficult."

32. Revert back.

Revert indicates returning to a former or earlier state. Something that reverts goes back to how it used to be. No need to add back.

33. (During the) course (of).

During means "in or throughout the duration of," and doesn't require the use of the word "course."

34. Same identical.

Same and identical means the same thing and should not be used together.

35. Completely filled/finished/opposite.

Completely indicates thoroughness. However, the words finished and filled already indicate something thoroughly filled or finished to the extent possible. The words filled and finished thus do not need to be qualified with "completely."

36. Since the time when.

In this phrase, 'the time when' is not necessary as 'since' already indicates sometime in the past.

37. Close proximity/scrutiny.

Proximity means being close, in respect to location. Scrutiny means studying something closely. Both words already suggest close, whether in respect to location as with proximity, or in respect to study, as with scrutiny. It is therefore unnecessary to use the words together.

38. Spell out in detail.

'Spell out' involves providing details, so no need to add "in detail."

39. Written down.

Anything written can be said to be taken down. Written should therefore be used on its own.

40. (Filled to) capacity.

Anything that is filled has reached its capacity and so the word capacity does not need to be used along with filled.

41. Unintended mistake.

Something is a mistake because it is not intended. The lack of intention is plain and so there is no need to qualify with "unintended."

42. Still remains.

"Remains" signifies that something is still as it is, and so using 'still' is superfluous.

43. Actual experience/fact.

Something becomes an experience after it has occurred. If it didn't occur it is not an experience. A fact is only a fact when it is sure or confirmed. Both experience and fact thus do not need to be modified with "actual."

44. Therapeutic treatment.

Therapeutic refers to the healing or curing of illness. By nature all medical treatment is therapeutic in that it aims to heal or cure. When speaking of medical treatment, there is thus no need to use therapeutic to qualify treatment.

45. At the present time.

"At present" alone indicates the present time or "at this time." Using "at the present time" is the verbose version. Better to just use "at present."

46. Unexpected surprise.

A surprise is unexpected by nature. The unexpected nature is assumed once the word surprised is read or heard. No need to use unexpected to qualify it.

47. As for example.

"As" indicates the use of an example and so it is redundant to say "an example."

48. Usual custom.

A custom refers to something that is observed or done repeatedly or routinely. The use of 'usual' along with custom is not necessary.

49. Added bonus.

Bonus already indicates something extra, in addition to the ordinary. Using "added" to describe the bonus is not necessary.

50. Few in number.

Something is few because it is small in number. No need to use number with few.

How to Prepare for a Test

MOST STUDENTS HIDE THEIR HEADS AND PROCRASTINATE WHEN FACED WITH PREPARING FOR AN EXAMINATION, HOPING THAT SOMEHOW THEY WILL BE SPARED THE AGONY OF TAKING THAT TEST, ESPECIALLY IF IT IS A BIG ONE THAT THEIR FUTURES RELY ON. Avoiding the all-important test is what many students do best and unfortunately, they suffer the consequences because of their lack of preparation.

Test preparation requires strategy. It also requires a dedication to getting the job done. It is the perfect training ground for anyone planning a professional life. Besides having several reliable strategies, the wise student also has a clear goal in mind and knows how to accomplish it. These tried and true concepts have worked well and will make your test preparation easier.

The Study Approach.

Take responsibility for your own test preparation.

It is a common- but big - mistake to link your studying to someone else's. Study partners are great, but only if they are reliable. It is your job to be prepared for the test, even if a study partner fails you. Do not allow others to distract you from your goals.

Prioritize the time available to study.

When do you learn best, early in the day or in the dark of night? Does your mind absorb and retain information most efficiently in small blocks of time, or do you require long stretches to get the most done? It is important to figure out the best blocks of time available to you when you can be the most productive. Try to consolidate activities to allow for longer periods of study time.

Find a quiet place where you will not be disturbed.

Do not try to squeeze in quality study time in any old location. Find some place peaceful and with a minimum of distractions, such as the library, a park or even the laundry room. Good lighting is essential and you need to have comfortable seating and a desk surface large enough to hold your materials. It is probably not a great idea to study in your bedroom. You might be distracted by clothes on the floor, a book you have been planning to read, the telephone or something else. Besides, in the middle of studying, that bed will start to look very comfortable. Whatever you do, avoid using the bed as a place to study since you might fall asleep to avoid your work! That is the last thing that you should be doing during study time.

The exception is flashcards. By far the most productive study time is sitting down and studying and studying only. However, with flashcards you can carry them with you and make use of odd moments, like standing in line or waiting for the bus. This isn't as productive, but it really helps and is definately worth doing.

Determine what you need to study.

Gather together your books, your notes, your laptop and any other materials needed to focus on your study for this exam. Ensure you have everything you need so you don't waste time. Remember paper, pencils and erasers, sticky notes, bottled water and a snack. Keep your phone with you if you need it to find out essential information, but keep it turned off so others can't distract you.

Have a positive attitude.

It is essential that you approach your studies for the test with an attitude that says you will pass it. And pass it with flying colors! This is one of the most important keys to successful study strategy. Believing that you are capable actually helps you to become capable.

THE STRATEGY OF STUDYING

Make materials easy to review and access.

Consolidate materials to help keep your study area clutter free. If you have a laptop and a means of getting on line, you do not need a dictionary and thesaurus as well since those things are easily accessible via the internet. Go through written notes and consolidate those, as well. Have everything you need, but do not weigh yourself down with duplicates.

Review class notes.

Stay on top of class notes and assignments by reviewing them frequently. Re-writing notes can be a terrific study trick, as it helps lock in information. Pay special attention to any comments that have been made by the teacher. If a study guide has been made available as part of the class materials, use it! It will be a valuable tool to use for studying.

Estimate how much time you will need.

If you are concerned about the amount of time you have available it is a good idea to set up a schedule so that you do not get bogged down on one section and end without enough time left to study other things. Remember to schedule break time, and use that time for a little exercise or other stress reducing techniques.

Test yourself to determine your weaknesses.

Look online for additional assessment and evaluation tools available for a particular subject. Once you have determined areas of concern, you will be able to focus on studying the information they contain and just brush up on the other areas of the exam.

Mental Prep – How to Psych Yourself Up for a Test

Because tests contribute mightily to your final class grade or to whether you are accepted into a program, it is understandable that taking tests can create a great deal of anxiety for many students. Even students who know they have learned all the required material find their minds going blank as they stare at the words in the questions. One easy way to overcome that anxiety is to prepare mentally for the test. Mentally preparing for an exam is really not difficult. There are simple techniques that any student can learn to increase their chances of earning a great score on the day of the test.

Do not procrastinate.

Study the material for the test when it becomes available, and continue to review the material until the test day. By waiting until the last minute and trying to cram for the test the night before, you actually increase the amount of anxiety you feel. This leads to an increase in negative self-talk. Telling yourself "I can't learn this. I am going to fail" is a pretty sure indication that you are right. At best, your performance on the test will not be as strong if you have procrastinated instead of studying.

Positive self-talk.

Positive self-talk serves both to drown out negative self-talk and to increase your confidence in your abilities. Whenever you begin feeling overwhelmed or anxious about the test, remind yourself that you have studied enough, you know the material and that you will pass the test. Use only positive words. Both negative and positive self-talk are really just your fantasy, so why not choose to be a winner?

Do not compare yourself to anyone else.

Do not compare yourself to other students, or your performance to theirs. Instead, focus on your own strengths and weaknesses and prepare accordingly. Regardless of how others perform, your performance is the only one that matters to your grade. Comparing yourself to others increases your anxiety and your level of negative self-talk before the test.

Visualize.

Make a mental image of yourself taking the test. You know the answers and feel relaxed. Visualize doing well on the test and having no problems with the material. Visualizations can increase your confidence and decrease the anxiety you might otherwise feel before the test. Instead of thinking of this as a test, see it as an opportunity to demonstrate what you have learned!

Avoid negativity.

Worry is contagious and viral - once it gets started it builds on itself. Cut it off before it gets to be a problem. Even if you are relaxed and confident, being around anxious, worried classmates might cause you to start feeling anxious. Before the test, tune out the fears of classmates. Feeling anxious and worried before an exam is normal, and every student experiences those feelings at some point. However, you cannot allow these feelings to interfere with your ability to perform well. Practicing mental preparation techniques and remembering that the test is not the only measure of your academic performance will ease your anxiety and ensure that you perform at your best.

How to Take a Test

Everyone knows that taking an exam is stressful, but it does not have to be that bad! There are a few simple things that you can do to increase your score on any type of test. Take a look at these tips and consider how you can incorporate them into your study time.

Reading the Instructions

This is the most basic point, but one that, surprisingly, many students ignore and it can cost them big time! Since reading the instructions is one of the most common, and 100% preventable mistakes, we have a whole section just on reading instructions.

Pay close attention to the sample questions. Almost all standardized tests offer sample questions, paired with their correct solutions. Go through these to make sure that you understand what they mean and how they arrived at the correct answer. Do not be afraid to ask the test supervisor for help with a sample that confuses you, or instructions that you are unsure of.

Tips for Reading the Question

We could write pages and pages of tips just on reading the test questions. Here are the ones that will help you the most.

- **Think first.** Before you look at the answer, read and think about the question. It is best to try to come up with the correct answer before you look at the options given. This way, when the test-writer tries to trick you with a close answer, you will not fall for it.

- **Make it true or false.** If a question confuses you, then look at each answer option and think of it as a "true" "false" question. Select the one that seems most likely to be "true."

- **Mark the Question.** For some reason, a lot of test-takers are afraid to mark up their test booklet. Unless you are specifically told not to mark in the booklet, you should feel free to use it to your advantage. More on this below.

- **Circle Key Words.** As you are reading the question, underline or circle key words. This helps you to focus on the most critical information needed to solve the problem. For example, if the question said, "Which of these is not a synonym for huge?" You might circle "not," "synonym" and "huge." That clears away the clutter and lets you focus on what is important.

- **Always underline these words:** all, none, always, never, most, best, true, false and except.

- **Cross out irrelevant choices.** If you find yourself confused by lengthy questions, cross out anything that you think is irrelevant, obviously wrong, or information that you think is offered to distract you.

- **Do not try to read between the lines.** Usually, questions are written to be straightforward, with no deep, underlying meaning. The simple answer really is often the correct answer. Do not over-analyze!

How to Take a Test - The Basics

Some tests are designed to assess your ability to quickly grab the necessary information; this type of exam makes speed a priority. Others are more concerned with your depth of knowledge, and how accurate it is. When you receive a test, look it over to determine whether the test is for speed or accuracy. If the test is for speed, like many standardized tests, your strategy is clear; answer as many questions as quickly as possible.

Watch out, though! There are a few tests that are designed to determine how fully and accurately you can answer the questions. Guessing on this type of test is a big mistake, because the teacher expects any student with an average grade to be able to complete the test in the time given. Racing through the test and making guesses that prove to be incorrect will cost you big time!

Every little bit helps.

If you are permitted calculators, or other materials, make sure you bring them, even if you do not think you will need them. Use everything at your disposal to increase your score.

Make time your friend.

Budget your time from the moment your pencil hits the page until you are finished with the exam, and stick to it! Virtually all standardized tests have a time limit for each section. The amount of time you are permitted for each portion of the test will almost certainly be included in the instructions or printed at the top of the page. If for some reason it is not immediately visible, rather than wasting your time hunting for it you can use the points or percentage of the score as a proxy to make an educated guess regarding the time limit.

Use the allotted time for each section and then move onto the next section whether you have completed the first section or not. Stick with the instructions and you will be able to answer most the questions in each section.

With speed tests you may not be able to complete the entire test. Rest assured that you are not really expected to! The goal of this type of examination is to determine how quickly you can reach into your brain and access a particular piece of information, which is one way of determining how well you know it. If you know a test you are taking is a speed test, you will know the strategies to use for the best results.

Easy does it.

One smart way to tackle a test is to locate the easy questions and answer those first. This is a time-tested strategy that never fails, because it saves you a lot of unnecessary fretting. First, read the question and decide if you can answer it in less than a minute. If so, complete the question and go to the next one. If not, skip it for now and continue to the next question. By the time you have completed the first pass through this section of the exam, you will have answered a good number of questions. Not only does it boost your confidence, relieve anxiety and kick your memory up a notch, you will know exactly how many questions remain and can allot the rest of your time accordingly. Think of doing the easy questions first as a warm-up!

If you run out of time before you manage to tackle all the difficult questions, do not let it throw you. All that means is you have used your time in the most efficient way possible by answering as many questions correctly as you could. Missing a few points by not answering a question whose answer you do not know just means you spent that time answering one whose answer you did.

A word to the wise: Skipping questions for which you are drawing a complete blank is one thing, but we are not suggesting you skip every question you come across that you are not 100 % certain of. A good rule of thumb is to try to answer at least eight of every 10 questions the first time through.

Do not watch your watch.

At best, taking an important exam is an uncomfortable situation. If you are like most people, you might be tempted to subconsciously distract yourself from the task at hand. One of the most common ways to do so is by becoming obsessed with your watch or the wall clock Do not watch your watch! Take it off and place it on the top corner of your desk, far enough away that you will not be tempted to look at it every two minutes. Better still, turn the watch face away from you. That way, every time you try to sneak a peek, you will be reminded to refocus your attention to the task at hand. Give yourself permission to check your watch or the wall clock after you complete each section. If you know yourself to be a bit of a slow-poke in other aspects of life, you can check your watch a bit more often. Even so, focus on answering the questions, not on how many minutes have elapsed since you last looked at it.

Divide and conquer.

What should you do when you come across a question that is so complicated you may not even be certain what is being asked? As we have suggested, the first time through the section you are best off skipping the question. But at some point, you will need to return to it and get it under control. The best way to handle questions that leave you feeling so anxious you can hardly think is by breaking them into manageable pieces. Solving smaller bits is always easier. For complicated questions, divide them into bite-sized pieces and solve these smaller sets separately. Once you understand what the reduced sections are really saying, it will be much easier to put them together and get a handle on the bigger question.

Reason your way through the toughest questions.

If you find that a question is so dense you can't figure out how to break it into smaller pieces, there are a few strategies that might help. First, read the question again and look for hints. Can you re-word the question in one or more different ways? This may give you clues. Look for words that can function as either verbs or nouns, and try to figure out from the sentence structure which it is here. Remember that many nouns in English have several different meanings. While some of those meanings might be related, sometimes they are completely distinct. If reading the sentence one way does not make sense, consider a different definition or meaning for a key word.

The truth is, it is not always necessary to understand a question to arrive at a correct answer! A trick that successful students understand is using Strategy 5, Elimination. Frequently, at least one answer is clearly wrong and can be crossed off the list of possible correct answers. Next, look at the remaining answers and eliminate any that are only partially true. You may still have to flat-out guess from time to time, but using the process of elimination will help you make your way to the correct answer more often than not - even when you don't know what the question means!

Do not leave early.

Use all the time allotted to you, even if you can't wait to get out of the testing room. Instead, once you have finished, spend the remaining time reviewing your answers. Go back to those questions that were most difficult for you and review your response. Another good way to use this time is to return to multiple-choice questions in which you filled in a bubble. Do a spot check, reviewing every fifth or sixth question to make sure your answer coincides with the bubble you filled in. This is a great way to catch yourself if you made a mistake, skipped a bubble and therefore put all your answers in the wrong bubbles!

Become a super sleuth and look for careless errors. Look for questions that have double negatives or other odd phrasing; they might be an attempt to throw you off. Careless errors on your part might be the result of skimming a question and missing a key word. Words such as "always," "never," "sometimes," "rarely" and the like can give a strong indication of the answer the question is really seeking. Don't throw away points by being careless!

Just as you budgeted time at the beginning of the test to allow for easy and more difficult questions, be sure to budget sufficient time to review your answers. On essay questions and math questions where you are required to show your work, check your writing to make sure it is legible.

Math questions can be especially tricky. The best way to double check math questions is by figuring the answer using a different method, if possible.

Here is another terrific tip. It is likely that no matter how hard you try, you will have a handful of questions you just are not sure of. Keep them in mind as you read through the rest of the test. If you can't answer a question, looking back over the test to find a different question that addresses the same topic might give you clues.

We know that taking the test has been stressful and you can

hardly wait to escape. Just keep in mind that leaving before you double-check as much as possible can be a quick trip to disaster. Taking a few extra minutes can make the difference between getting a bad grade and a great one. Besides, there will be lots of time to relax and celebrate after the test is turned in.

In the Test Room – What you MUST do!

If you are like the rest of the world, there is almost nothing you would rather avoid than taking a test. Unfortunately, that is not an option if you want to pass. Rather than suffer, consider a few attitude adjustments that might turn the experience from a horrible one to...well, an interesting one! Take a look at these tips. Simply changing how you perceive the experience can change the experience itself.

Get in the mood.

After weeks of studying, the big day has finally arrived. The worst thing you can do to yourself is arrive at the test site feeling frustrated, worried, and anxious. Keep a check on your emotional state. If your emotions are shaky before a test it can determine how well you do on the test. It is extremely important that you pump yourself up, believe in yourself, and use that confidence to get in the mood!

Don't fight reality.

Oftentimes, students resent tests, and with good reason. After all, many people do not test well, and they know the grade they end with does not accurately reflect their true knowledge. It is easy to feel resentful because tests classify students and create categories that just don't seem fair. Face it: Students who are great at rote memorization and not that good at actually analyzing material often score higher than those who might be more creative thinkers and balk at simply memorizing cold, hard facts. It may not be fair, but there it is anyway. Conformity is an asset on tests, and creativity is often a liability. There is no point in wasting time or energy being upset about this reality. Your first step is to accept the reality and get used to it. You will get higher marks when you realize tests do count and that you must give them your best effort. Think about your future and the career that is easier to achieve if you have consistently earned high grades. Avoid negative energy and focus on anything that lifts your enthusiasm and increases your motivation.

Get there early enough to relax.

If you are wound up, tense, scared, anxious, or feeling rushed, it will cost you. Get to the exam room early and relax before you go in. This way, when the exam starts, you are comfortable and ready to apply yourself. Of course, you do not want to arrive so early that you are the only one there. That will not help you relax; it will only give you too much time to sit there, worry and get wound up all over again.

If you can, visit the room where you will be taking your exam a few days ahead of time. Having a visual image of the room can be surprisingly calming, because it takes away one of the big 'unknowns'. Not only that, but once you have visited, you know how to get there and will not be worried about getting lost. Furthermore, driving to the test site once lets you know how much time you need to allow for the trip. That means three potential stressors have been eliminated all at once.

Get it down on paper.

One of the advantages of arriving early is that it allows you time to recreate notes. If you spend a lot of time worrying about whether you will be able to remember information like names, dates, places, and mathematical formulas, there is a solution for that. Unless the exam you are taking allows you to use your books and notes, (and very few do) you will have to rely on memory. Arriving early gives to time to tap into your memory and jot down key pieces of information you know will be asked. Just make certain you are allowed to make notes once you are in the testing site; not all locations will permit it. Once you get your test, on a small piece of paper write down everything you are afraid you will forget. It will take a minute or two but by dumping your worries onto the page you have effectively eliminated a certain amount of anxiety and driven off the panic you feel.

Get comfortable in your chair.

Here is a clever technique that releases physical stress and helps you get comfortable, even relaxed in your body. You will tense and hold each of your muscles for just a few seconds. The trick is, you must tense them hard for the technique to work. You might want to practice this technique a few times at home; you do not want an unfamiliar technique to add to your stress just before a test, after all! Once you are at the test site, this exercise can always be done in the rest room or another quiet location.

Start with the muscles in your face then work down your body. Tense, squeeze and hold the muscles for a moment or two. Notice the feel of every muscle as you go down your body. Scowl to tense your forehead, pull in your chin to tense your neck. Squeeze your shoulders down to tense your back. Pull in your stomach all the way back to your ribs, make your lower back tight then stretch your fingers. Tense your leg muscles and calves then stretch your feet and your toes. You should be as stiff as a board throughout your entire body.

Now relax your muscles in reverse starting with your toes. Notice how all the muscles feel as you relax them one by one. Once you have released a muscle or set of muscles, allow them to remain relaxed as you proceed up your body. Focus on how you are feeling as all the tension leaves. Start breathing deeply when you get to your chest muscles. By the time you have found your chair, you will be so relaxed it will feel like bliss!

Fight distraction.

A lucky few are able to focus deeply when taking an important examination, but most people are easily distracted, probably because they would rather be anyplace else! There are a number of things you can do to protect yourself from distraction.

Stay away from windows. If you select a seat near a window you may end gazing out at the landscape instead of paying attention to the work at hand. Furthermore, any sign of human activity, from a single individual walking by to a couple having an argument or exchanging a kiss will draw your attention away from your important work. What goes on outside should not be allowed to distract you.

Choose a seat away from the aisle so you do not become distracted by people who leave early. People who leave the exam room early are often the ones who fail. Do not compare your time to theirs.

Of course, you love your friends; that's why they are your friends! In the test room, however, they should become complete strangers inside your mind. Forget they are there. The first step is to physically distance yourself from friends or classmates. That way, you will not be tempted to glance at them to see how they are doing, and there will be no chance of eye contact that could either distract you or even lead to an accusation of cheating. Furthermore, if they are feeling stressed because they did not spend the focused time studying that you did, their anxiety is less likely to permeate your hard-earned calm.

Of course, you will want to choose a seat where there is sufficient light. Nothing is worse than trying to take an important examination under flickering lights or dim bulbs.

Ask the instructor or exam proctor to close the door if there is a lot of noise outside. If the instructor or proctor is unable to do so, block out the noise as best you can. Do not let anything disturb you.

Make sure you have enough pencils, pens and whatever else you will need. Many entrance exams do not permit you to bring personal items such as candy bars into the testing room. If this is the case with the exam you are sitting for, be sure to eat a nutritionally balanced breakfast. Eat protein, complex carbohydrates and a little fat to keep you feeling full and to supercharge your energy. Nothing is worse than a sudden drop in blood sugar during an exam.

Do not allow yourself to become distracted by being too cold or hot. Regardless of the weather outside, carry a sweater, scarf or jacket if the air conditioning at the test site is set too high, or the heat set too low. By the same token, dress in layers so that you are prepared for a range of temperatures.

Bring a watch so that you can keep track of time management. The danger here is many students become obsessed with how many minutes have passed since the last question. Instead of wearing the watch, remove it and place it in the far upper corner of the desk with the face turned away. That way, you cannot become distracted by repeatedly glancing at the time, but it is available if you need to know it.

Drinking a gallon of coffee or gulping a few energy drinks might seem like a great idea, but it is, in fact, a very bad one. Caffeine, pep pills or other artificial sources of energy are more likely to leave you feeling rushed and ragged. Your brain might be clicking along, all right, but chances are good it is not clicking along on the right track! Furthermore, drinking lots of coffee or energy drinks will mean frequent trips to the rest room. This will cut into the time you should be spending answering questions and is a distraction in itself, since each time you need to leave the room you lose focus. Pep pills will only make it harder for you to think straight when solving complicated problems on the exam.

At the same time, if anxiety is your problem try to find ways around using tranquilizers during test-taking time. Even medically prescribed anti-anxiety medication can make you less alert and even decrease your motivation. Being motivated is what you need to get you through an exam. If your anxiety is so bad that it threatens to interfere with your ability to take an exam, speak to your doctor and ask for documentation. Many testing sites will allow non-distracting test rooms, extended testing time and other accommodations as long as a doctor's note that explains the situation is made available.

Keep Breathing.

It might not make a lot of sense, but when people become anxious, tense, or scared, their breathing becomes shallow and, in some cases, they stop breathing all together! Pay attention to your emotions, and when you are feeling worried, focus on your breathing. Take a moment to remind yourself to breathe deeply and regularly. Drawing in steady, deep breaths energizes the body. When you continue to breathe deeply you will notice you exhale all the tension.

It is a smart idea to rehearse breathing at home. With continued practice of this relaxation technique, you will begin to know the muscles that tense up under pressure. Call these your "signal muscles." These are the ones that will speak to you first, begging you to relax. Take the time to listen to those muscles and do as they ask. With just a little breathing practice, you will get into the habit of checking yourself regularly and when you realize you are tense, relaxation will become second nature.

AVOID ANXIETY BEFORE A TEST

Manage your time effectively.

This is a key to your success! You need blocks of uninterrupted time to study all the pertinent material. Creating and maintaining a schedule will help keep you on track, and will remind family members and friends that you are not available. Under no circumstances should you change your blocks of study time to accommodate someone else, or cancel a study session to do something more fun. Do not interfere with your study time for any reason!

Relax.

Use whatever works best for you to relieve stress. Some folks like a good, calming stretch with yoga, others find expressing themselves through journaling to be useful. Some hit the floor for a series of crunches or planks, and still others take a slow stroll around the garden. Integrate a little relaxation time into your schedule, and treat that time, too, as sacred.

Eat healthy.

Instead of reaching for the chips and chocolate, fresh fruits and vegetables are not only yummy but offer nutritional benefits that help to relieve stress. Some foods accelerate stress instead of reducing it and should be avoided. Foods that add to higher anxiety include artificial sweeteners, candy and other sugary foods, carbonated sodas, chips, chocolate, eggs, fried foods, junk foods, processed foods, red meat, and other foods containing preservatives or heavy spices. Instead, eat a bowl of berries and some yogurt!

Get plenty of ZZZZZZZs.

Do not cram or try to do an all-nighter. If you created a study schedule at the beginning, and if you have stuck with that schedule, have confidence! Staying up too late trying to cram in last-minute bits of information is going to leave you exhausted the next day. Besides, whatever new information you cram in will only displace all the important ideas you've spent weeks learning. Remember: You need to be alert and fully functional the day of the exam

Have confidence in yourself!

Everyone experiences some anxiety when taking a test, but exhibiting a positive attitude banishes anxiety and fills you with the knowledge you really do know what you need to know. This is your opportunity to show how well prepared you are. Go for it!

Be sure to take everything you need.

Depending on the exam, you may be allowed to have a pen or pencil, calculator, dictionary or scratch paper with you. Have these gathered together along with your entrance paperwork and identification so that you are sure you have everything that is needed.

Do not chitchat with friends.

Let your friends know ahead of time that it is not anything personal, but you are going to ignore them in the test room! You need to find a seat away from doors and windows, one that has good lighting, and get comfortable. If other students are worried their anxiety could be detrimental to you; of course, you do not have to tell your friends that. If you are afraid they will be offended, tell them you are protecting them from your anxiety!

Common Test-Taking Mistakes

Taking a test is not much fun at best. When you take a test and make a stupid mistake that negatively affects your grade, it is natural to be very upset, especially when it is something that could have been easily avoided. So what are some of the common mistakes that are made on tests?

Do not fail to put your name on the test.

How could you possibly forget to put your name on a test? You would be amazed at how often that happens. Very often, tests without names are thrown out immediately, resulting in a failing grade.

Marking the wrong multiple-choice answer.

It is important to work at a steady pace, but that does not mean bolting through the questions. Be sure the answer you are marking is the one you mean to. If the bubble you need to fill in or the answer you need to circle is 'C', do not allow yourself to get distracted and select 'B' instead.

Answering a question twice.

Some multiple-choice test questions have two very similar answers. If you are in too much of a hurry, you might select them both. Remember that only one answer is correct, so if you choose more than one, you have automatically failed that question.

Mishandling a difficult question.

We recommend skipping difficult questions and returning to them later, but beware! First, be certain that you do return to the question. Circling the entire passage or placing a large question mark beside it will help you spot it when you are reviewing your test. Secondly, if you are not careful to skip the question, you can mess yourself up badly. Imagine that a question is too difficult and you decide to save it for later. You read the next question, which you know the answer to, and you fill in that answer. You continue to the end of the test then return to the difficult question only to discover you didn't actually skip it! Instead, you inserted the answer to the following question in the spot reserved for the harder one, thus throwing off the remainder of your test!

Incorrectly Transferring an answer from scratch paper.

This can happen easily if you are trying to hurry! Double check any answer you have figured out on scratch paper, and make sure what you have written on the test itself is an exact match!

Don't ignore the clock, and don't marry it, either.

In a timed examination many students lose track of the time and end up without sufficient time to complete the test. Remember to pace yourself! At the same time, though, do not allow yourself to become obsessed with how much time has elapsed, either.

Thinking too much.

Oftentimes, your first thought is your best thought. If you worry yourself into insecurity, your self-doubts can trick you into choosing an incorrect answer when your first impulse was the right one!

Be prepared.

Running out of ink and not having an extra pen or pencil is not an excuse for failing an exam! Have everything you need, and have extras. Bring tissue, an extra eraser, several sharpened pencils, batteries for electronic devices, and anything else you might need.

Not following directions.

Directions are carefully worded. If you skim directions, it is very easy to miss key words or misinterpret what is being said. Nothing is worse than failing an examination simply because you could not be bothered with reading the instructions!

Conclusion

CONGRATULATIONS! You have made it this far because you have applied yourself diligently to practicing for the exam and no doubt improved your potential score considerably! Passing your up-coming exam is a huge step in a journey that might be challenging at times but will be many times more rewarding and fulfilling. That is why being prepared is so important.

Good Luck!

Register for Free Updates and More Practice Test Questions

Register your purchase at

www.test-preparation.ca/strategy.html for fast and convenient access to updates, errata, free test tips and more practice test questions.

Endnotes

Reading comprehension passages where noted below are used in modified form under the Creative Commons Attribution-ShareAlike 3.0 License. For details visit,

http://en.wikipedia.org/wiki/Wikipedia:Text_of_Creative_Commons_Attribution-ShareAlike_3.0_Unported_License

[1] What is Free Range Chicken In *Answers.com*. Retrieved Feb 14, 2009, from http://wiki.answers.com/Q/What_is_free-range_chicken.
[2] Grizzly Bear. In *Wikipedia*. Retrieved Feb 14, 2009, from http://en.wikipedia org/wiki/Grizzly_Bear.
[3] Grizzly Polar Bear Hybrid. In *Wikipedia*. Retrieved Feb 14, 2009, from http://en.wikipedia.org/wiki/Grizzly%E2%80%93polar_bear_hybrid.
[4] Peafowl. In *Wikipedia*. Retrieved Feb 14, 2009, from en.wikipedia.org/wiki/Peafowl.
[5] Smallpox. In *Wikipedia*. Retrieved Feb 14, 2009, from http://en.wikipedia.org/wiki/Smallpox.
[6] Lightning. In *Wikipedia*. Retrieved Feb 14, 2009, from http://en.wikipedia.org/wiki/Lightning.
[7] Venus. In *Wikipedia*. Retrieved Feb 14, 2009, from http://en.wikipedia.org/wiki/Venus.
[8] Weather. In *Wikipedia*. Retrieved Feb 14, 2009, from http://en.wikipedia.org/wiki/Weather.

www.ingramcontent.com/pod-product-compliance
Lightning Source LLC
Chambersburg PA
CBHW071822080526
44589CB00012B/891